Undisturbed: A Guide To Emotional Wellness

Adam Oakley

Copyright

www.InnerPeaceNow.com

www.AdamOakleyWriting.com

ISBN-13: 978-1502480606
ISBN-10: 1502480603

Contents

Introduction – Discarding Conditioning 1

Part 1 - What They Told You Wasn't True 3

Emotions Are Not Personal 4

Thoughts or Reality? 8

Don't Be Faithful To Suffering 11

Dissolving The Painmaker 13

The Myth Of Resistance 15

The Trick Of Suppression 18

Don't Have An Ideal Self..23

Dissolving Boredom..26

The Cheat Of Jealousy...28

Undoing Loneliness...30

No Worries..32

Part 2 - How-To's..34

How To Stop Being Concerned About Other People's
Opinions 35

How To Deal With Anxiety...41

How To Deal With Conflict...46

How To Deal With Pain 55

How To Deal With Depression 59

How To Transcend Suffering 64

How To Forgive..68

Part 3 - Discovering Freedom 74

The Futility Of Regret...75

Eradicating Guilt...77

Healing Anger 81

Dissolving Fear 86

Undisturbed Being...88

Embracing Life Energy...90

The Stages And Process Of Emotional Healing............92

About The Author 102

Introduction – Discarding Conditioning

The aim is not to stop feeling emotions. Let all emotions come. This book aims to show that emotions are not wrong or bad, and need not be clung to or given such great importance. Emotions are fleeting, they are not meant to be held and kept, they are energy movements that come and go. To hold and cling on to emotions is a habit of the human mind, and it ends up creating great inner turmoil.

We can read spiritual or self-help books, listen to different teachers, and often a theme is to be at peace, cool and calm. Then, if we feel an emotion, such as anger or some kind of resistance, we can end up resisting the experience even more, since the mind believes it is "bad" or "should not be happening". Enough conditioning, spiritual or otherwise. Forget what you have learned about emotion.

If you were to forget what you think you know about emotions, if you were completely empty, had no assumptions that the emotions are who you are, and had no assumption that emotions need to be figured out or resisted, then this book would not be needed. This book aims to help you allow yourself to just be empty – an empty space in which emotion can come and go, rather than a solid-feeling person that sticks to emotions and suffers them. Even all useful spiritual guidance points you to no longer judge emotions. They point you to natural emptiness, natural un-knowingness. In this inner space, negative and futile reactions are no longer sustained, and so can be released naturally.

To be free from something, you give the thing freedom to *be*. The same can be said for emotions. Give up the fight, withdraw the belief that you should feel different, withdraw "you" altogether so that rather than the experience being personal and "yours", it is just an experience arising, affecting no-one.

Surrender to emotions without reservation. Let them *be*. Then what is useful remains, what is useless or harmful becomes dissolved. This takes place by itself when you allow inner trouble without resisting it. No longer believe what you have been told about emotions, no longer believe what your mind says about them, and no longer believe what the emotion says about itself. Go back to basics, just be aware of what happens. See that whatever you can perceive, including thoughts, personality and emotions, are all movements that happen by themselves – they are not who you are, nor are they yours to police. You are the awareness itself, which remains undisturbed. In the midst of inner trouble, your nonresistance dissolves it. You can allow yourself to remain undisturbed. Nonresistance and nonjudgement are what burn up old pain most quickly and effectively, and set you free, whether emotion is there or not.

So, simply give up the burden of analysis and control. No longer argue with inner disturbances. They all arise in an undisturbed awareness.

Part 1

What They Told You Wasn't True

Part 1, and in fact the whole book, is attempting to show you that the way we have been taught to think and treat our feelings, is completely ineffective. There is a more efficient way of treating ourselves, which is not weakness, but sanity.

Not many humans have really known how to be happy, many people have suffered from their own minds, and this gets passed on down the generations. Often we have had parents that simply believe Life should be an ordeal of suffering, as if that's just the way it is, and your experience should be no different. No one is to blame, but let's not go along with the charade of suffering any longer...

Emotions Are Not Personal

"No longer 'have' emotions. No longer own them. No longer identify with these energies that arise in the awareness that you are. Let them be. They arise by themselves, they are not yours to regulate or police."

They claim to be personal, but are they really? If you just observe your inner state - whatever emotions come or go - do so of their own accord. There is not a person inside that says: "ok, now I'm going to get angry" or "ok, I command anxiety to come". No - they arise by themselves. They are energy movements. What gives them their strength is our *belief* that they are personal. Belief is everything. We overlook its power, but it is obvious that whatever you believe - is true for you. This is massively significant in determining suffering or lack of it. Your whole experience of the world is affected by what you do or do not believe. Two people's experiences could be vastly different just from believing or not believing in one thought.

Is this not some kind of relief? That the emotions you experience are not yours to manage? They are not who you are. They are not your responsibility - you may have noticed that they are very difficult to control. All of our frustration and confusion come when we believe we are the ones producing these emotions, yet they seem to have some uncontrollable force behind them. This can make negative emotions create a kind of inner hell for us.

So let this be your realisation - that emotions are nothing to do with who you are. You are aware of them, but you do not personally create them. There is an energy in us that enjoys creating emotions and seeks to maintain them - we will get on to this later. See the impermanence of emotions, that they come and go, that they seem to have a will of their own. They can be triggered by certain events or they can come up unexpectedly. If you take ownership of them as if "I should stop feeling anxious" or "I should stop getting angry" - or whatever - then you can get into a mess and end up suppressing things which can do more harm than good. Notice how emotions rise and fall by themselves, without personal volition. You are the awareness in which they move.

Why Do They Feel So Personal?

Emotions feel personal because they are tied to a personal identity. From birth we are conditioned into taking ourselves to be separate people, separate personalities living in bodies. The personality is only the surface aspect of yourself. Have you ever looked a little deeper? How can the personality exist in the first place? Where does it come from? From where does it arise? Is it actually real, or just a bundle of thoughts and automatic behaviours?

What we believe to be our real identity as a separate person, is made up of imagination. It is a construction of thoughts. Even "I" or "me", in itself, is a thought.

With this formation of the imaginary inner person, also known as the separate "I" or "the ego", - a great deal of thought and emotion arises, all based around this central thought of "I". This "I" claims to be the thinker of thoughts and the producer of emotions, so we believe that the thoughts and emotions that arise are our own doing.

But are they your own doing? Do you choose to think, or does thinking happen by itself? Do you choose to feel angry, or sad, or calm, or happy, or do these feelings arise by themselves? For the most part, emotion and thoughts are playing in our awareness, by themselves. If we knew ourselves as the awareness in which all thought, emotion and personality arises, then we would naturally be undisturbed and at peace. Thought, emotion and personality would be in service to us, rather than dominating our experience of Life.

The real disturbance comes when we identify with the inner person, who is very involved in all the inner noise. This imaginary person enjoys the pleasant feelings, and suffers the painful ones, it is responsible for inner turmoil, yet feels a victim of it.

So, in a sense, nothing is personal, since it all happens by itself. The person "doing all of it" is an illusion, simply a creation of thought. It is a false self. Yet, because of this inner person absorbing so much belief and attention, it seems emotions and thoughts are "yours". See what happens if you can let thought and emotion be there, without calling them "yours". You will see that a voice in the head speaks, analyses and commentates, emotions come and go, all by themselves. They arise in the space of awareness, which is who you are.

There's Nothing Wrong With You

"You are awareness, not an object that rises in awareness."

It naturally follows that whatever emotions or thoughts you experience – does not imply that there is anything right or wrong with *you*. It could be said that there is an inner dysfunction that loves to create suffering – and this is part of the human condition – but it is not who you are in essence.

"I can't stop having these terrible thoughts", "I can't stop feeling anxious", "I can't stop thinking!" – all such thoughts are voices of the Painmaker – the energy field in humans that loves to create suffering. Be aware of yourself as the awareness in which dysfunction, noise or any insanity arises. This natural, ever-present yet non-objective awareness, when recognised, is the emergence of sanity, the end of the domination of the thinking mind.

We often think awareness must be a thing. If there is a painful emotion inside or a lot of noisy thoughts, we can be tricked by the mind that says "I have lost awareness". You haven't lost awareness. Awareness can not be lost. If you are aware that there is a lot of inner noise or emotion rising up – then that is enough. The only other thing is to stop arguing with it. Give up your fight with the inner state. The thoughts and emotions that make us suffer are based on conflict and resistance. They are in themselves, forms of resistance.

The antidote is no more conflict. Don't fight the fighter. Don't resist resistance. Without resisting your inner state, without calling it good or bad, without wishing it be different – you become more effortless, and it is easier to see that you *already* are the awareness in which these inner energies move.

The Sufferer

The inner person that seems to suffer thoughts and emotions, is not who you are. The person, or the sufferer, is only another thought. The inner person that suffers pain, is part of the pain itself. The inner person that seems to be dominated by thoughts, is part of the thoughts themselves. You are not a person, the feeling of a person arises IN you.

Be aware that the content of your mind, however potent or turbulent, arises in an untouched space. Surrender to the content, let it be, welcome it even, and it is easier to sense that rather than being the thought of "I" that arises as the mind, you are the untouched space, the impersonal source from which the inner person and its related thoughts arise.

<u>Thoughts or Reality?</u>

"This chapter may seem a bit philosophical, but the basic message is this: our thoughts often create unjust and unnecessary suffering for us. Thoughts are ok, but when given great importance and belief, they begin to cause trouble."

Be aware how much of your suffering comes from thoughts *about* things, rather than the things themselves. Do not be fooled by the mind. Humans have a habit of experiencing the senses with an added world of unnecessary interpretations and concepts, which can create vast amounts of suffering, for themselves and others. If there is no thought, does the problem or troubling situation even exist? Most of the problems we think we have, are merely creations of thought that are taken to be real.

Be aware of how often you view the world of thoughts, rather than the actual world. If you are thinking about what has happened, or what might happen, thoughts have taken over. If you are telling a story about what is happening now, thoughts have taken over. If you are thinking about someone else, thoughts have taken over. If you are thinking about yourself, thoughts have taken over. If you are thinking about your Life, thoughts have taken over. These thoughts have their place for practical purposes, but usually the attention of the human being is so completely absorbed by thinking, that we no longer see things as they are. We look at the conceptual version of the world, which differs in each person according to conditioning and personality. Thoughts have replaced reality for many of us. The mind labels everything, gives everything a name, and we become trapped in a conceptual world, without even realising it.

A basic example is a tree. If you look at a tree, often it will be overlooked. The mind says, "it's just a tree". The mind creates a label, and assigns it to an object. But in reality, it is not a tree, this is just something we have made up. A tree does not call itself a tree. This label is just something the human mind has created for communication purposes, but it has now been mistaken for the actual reality. Have you ever really looked at a tree, without calling it anything? If you simply look at it, without needing to add thought, you sense the reality of it. You sense the Life within it, the truth of "the tree" which is masked by the mental label. In the same way, mental labels can completely mask us from the truth of Life. We begin to believe the mind's labels are the truth of things. This is how we become tricked. The stories we tell about Life, our interpretations of events, are merely a bundle of thoughts. If you can see this, and that most of the time, these illusory thoughts create trouble, you will give them less respect, less importance, and the truth will emerge by itself.

This is most relevant for this book, because a great deal of human suffering is self-created. All tendencies such as anxiety, worry, problem-making, depression, guilt or hatred, are all creations of thought! Since we unquestionably take thoughts to represent truth, we suffer when the thoughts become dysfunctional.

Obsessive thinking carries on until we begin to question the truth of thoughts and what they claim to represent. Are they true? Do they fairly represent Life, or are they false interpretations? Are they serving you in this moment, or are they just draining energy? Are they in fact based on what you have been told by other people, rather than a reliable resource? What would be a reliable resource anyway? Even in the realm of science, what we call "facts" are often later disproved, and another "fact" replaces it. We try so hard to understand Life, how it works, but really we can't - it just turns into more thoughts and the mind says "this is how it is".

Distinguish between events as they happen, and the thoughts about them. See how there is a difference. The event is as it is. The thoughts that come of "me", "he", "she", "this" and "that" are all extra additions. They always claim to help, to enhance our understanding, but they create a limitation. They even enhance suffering. Thoughts *are* limitations. Often they create a *false* understanding, creating an illusory barrier between the present moment and our sense of self. The present moment is a unified whole, which through thinking, becomes fragmented into separate events and individuals in the mind. Without thought, what is an event? Without thought, who are you?

Thought is useful for creative purposes, for practical means, but the tool we call the mind is no longer a tool for many of us, it is the boss. Many people's waking lives are completely tyrannised by thinking, dominated by the concept of time, and everyone is looking to get away. We watch TV, crave company and stimulation, become obsessed with activity, drink or even do drugs, just to get away from the thoughts in the head.

There is a natural way. Start by realising that a world of concepts has been created by the mind. Everything is an idea! Everything from "me" and "other people" to what has happened and what might happen – are all just thoughts! No longer take thoughts so seriously.

Then there are the deeper emotions, the feelings that seem etched inside, creating suffering. Drop your arguments. Stop trying to mask your emotions or get rid of your feelings. No longer resist disturbance or trouble, welcome it. Whatever you accept, without judging it, without pushing away, no longer commands power over you. It begins to dissolve, since it is no longer being fed through your resistance. Inner disturbances seek to disturb. To let them disturb, to give up the fight, means they have no more reason to stay. Through nonresistance, you become aware that as well as the emotion being there, as well as the associated thoughts and identity, there is an untouched, empty space in which all arises, which is one with who you are.

Don't Be Faithful To Suffering

"We tend to give great value and importance to our painful emotions, we seem to give great belief and importance to what makes us suffer. We are somehow addicted to it. Don't give such faith to what hurts. See how it feels to no longer contribute to that which internally disturbs. If you relinquish your faith in the painful, a more peaceful quality can emerge."

Painful or troubling emotions really call for your attention. They demand that they be valued. We unquestioningly seem to give all of our belief and a great deal of importance to anything that limits or disturbs us. Whether it is upset, or a sense of lack or limitation, we feed these things in ourselves by taking them seriously, by believing them to be real. They are actually frauds. Troubling thoughts or emotions are usually part of the game of the personal self, to make you believe that the world or other people are the cause of your emotional suffering, rather than the personal self actually being the cause. The personal self (or "the ego") creates thoughts of this or that, he or she, this or that event, and then endows the thoughts with heaviness or some kind of disturbance. So really the trouble comes from the thoughts alone, not the actual external circumstances or objects.

We are then forever in a trap of trying to resolve or control everything externally so that we can once again be free or at ease. This never ends. You resolve one thing, feel better, then another thing comes up. The shortcut to peace is to no longer be loyal to what hurts. If suffering is created inside, why do we give such belief to it? Watch that it is self-created suffering – see the madness of it. If anything, the tendency to worship suffering in ourselves just maintains external situations of a similar frequency, or causes them to re-emerge in our lives.

Don't fight any of it, this would mean you take it seriously. Just let it be, but don't give the worries and trouble such importance. The thoughts and emotions act as if they know what the world is, as if they know what will or won't happen, and what is good or bad - but all of this is untrue. If you are suffering, you can be sure that the thoughts or emotions creating it are not trustworthy.

Action can still naturally take place, but it is intuitive, not so contaminated by a resistive little entity, but rather flowing from Life itself.

Dissolving The Painmaker

"The human dysfunction is an addiction to pain and suffering. There is an energy field that lives in many of us that loves to create problems, drama and conflict. Once you can recognise this energy in yourself – The Painmaker – you no longer identify with it. You see it is part of the human condition, which is not who you are. Allow it without judging it. In this way its hold will weaken."

We don't tend to have problems with "good" emotions i.e. pleasant emotions. There are not many people suffering from happiness. Where we suffer is when the denser, heavier emotions arise – such as fear, anxiety, depression, hatred or anger. These are resistive emotions, and resistance *is* suffering.

Have you ever noticed that you can be taken over by a certain emotion or feeling of inner suffering, almost as if it has a kind of repetitive cycle? Certain events or sometimes nothing in particular, will cause an intense emotional reflex, which seems completely out of proportion, out of control, and quite unpleasant?

Humans are often born with a strange addiction to suffering. You can notice in others and in yourself – that something seeks upset, enjoys disturbance and pain, loves to experience drama. This is what Eckhart Tolle has named the "Pain Body". For copyright reasons, if nothing else, we will refer to this entity as the Painmaker – an energy linked to the personal mind that creates suffering and enjoys it.

The troubling, persistent emotions that cause suffering for humans are all aspects of the Painmaker. Whether it is anxiety, resentment, frustration, dread, depression or anything else negative, it is produced and maintained by that which believes negativity is both useful and enjoyable.

Again, it is not personal, it is just an energy field that lives off of suffering, particularly emotional, but it can also use physical suffering to maintain and renew itself.

Noticing this addiction is a very valuable step. To see that something is on the lookout for pain, that it enjoys the feeling of suffering – is enough to break your identification with it. This weakens it. The step after this is to go completely counter-intuitive and no longer fight it. Let it be. Welcome it, even. This creates an inner environment of surrender, of non-resistance, which the Painmaker cannot survive in. It can only stay alive and cause trouble when you resist it, when you wish it were not there. To let it *be* without trying to change it, without analysing it, and without believing it is who you are, is like poison for the Painmaker.

So whenever you feel a certain negative emotion, whether it is a palpable rush of intense energy, or if it is a background sadness or discontent, be aware that it is not you. The pain energy has arisen, and is charging thoughts with the same pain. The thoughts of "I" and "me" (which are mental creations, rather than your true Self) are all charged with a similar frequency of pain. Simply see it as an energy field seeking renewal, nothing more.

The worst part about unhappiness, depression, fear or anything else is our aversion to these feelings, rather than the feelings themselves. Our desire for the emotion to be gone is what creates so much trouble. However you feel – accept it. Accept unhappiness, accept fear or anxiety, without labeling them, without calling them good or bad. Instantly, when you accept the feelings, they are not so bad. There is some space around them. This welcoming space is the space of healing, and the negative emotions can no longer be fueled by resistance.

The Myth Of Resistance

"We learn that the best way to deal with anything undesirable or unpleasant, is to resist. We believe resistance is what helps resolve the situation. For the most part, the painful tendency to resist life creates undesirable circumstances, sustains them longer, and keeps us trapped in the limited personal self.

To relinquish resistance and judgment brings forth a healing presence that also sustains useful action. This is the power of surrender."

Whenever an undesirable situation turns up, one that doesn't fit in with our minds' often rigid expectations, we feel it is only right to resist the situation. An undesirable situation could be anything from an external circumstance, to an unpleasant emotion, to a troubling thought. We believe that the way to resolve these disturbances is to resist, even to fight them, until they go away.

Try a different method - nonresistance. Try it on small things to start with. Give surrender a chance, as a kind of life-experiment. Surrender is to offer no resistance, to accept instead of reject, to say yes internally to what the present moment presents. It is to align yourself with Life and to reduce suffering. The most extreme and potent form of surrender is to accept this moment and its content as if you had chosen it. Sounds crazy, but miraculous in its consequences of healing, action and peace.

So whatever you feel - pain, a noisy mind, anger, hate, frustration, anxiety - no longer fight them. Accept them fully, without wishing that they were different, without trying to get over them or move past them. Have no expectation, no personal will, just allow them.

With this comes peace, and an inner environment in which all negative, resistive emotions can not survive. Surrendering to what happens outside you is also liberating. You are no longer heavily affected, no longer internally dominated by externals. Without offering resistance, you don't turn things into mental problems, and so your ability to act in the world is greatly enhanced. You remain clear and spacious rather than resistive and internally claustrophobic.

You also no longer feed undesirable situations with the energy of resistance. Resistance keeps whatever you are resisting alive, it makes the "problem" seem more real and more potent.

We are so used to being taught that resistance is the most effective way to get things done. Often we can even believe thoughts that say: "if I surrender, if I am then at peace, how will anything get done?". Try it - stuff still gets done, but you may find yourself wasting less energy. The moment uses you rather than you using it. You are no longer stuck fighting Life. Where situations would have triggered a fearful mind into taking action, you may now just remain silent. Silence and surrender have more useful effects on events and our surroundings than we realise. Or, you find yourself taking action, but you are not in as much inner trauma or conflict than if you were internally resisting.

Surrender may not seem easy at first, so don't be hard on yourself if it seems you can not relinquish inner resistance to what *is*. What *is*, is your direct experience at this moment, rather than the mental story of what is happening. With that said, if the mental story arises, if thoughts, emotions or sensations are there - all of these things are also part of what *is*. They are the direct experience of this moment. These energies are experienced without resistance or interpretation, not labeled as good or bad, and they are allowed to be there. The mind will say that this will mean the unpleasantness of Life will then take you over, based on the belief that "allowance is weakness". In fact, the unpleasantness is less potent, less severe, less disturbing. The mental idea of a person who can suffer things begins to fall away, and your actions take on a deeper power where necessary.

Resistance is habitual, and so it seems difficult to relinquish at first. You don't really have any choice in the matter – emotion and resistance are often one and the same. When resistance arises in you, surrender to this as well. Even this resistance is not who you are – it arises by itself, and is usually tied into a mind-made identity. Don't worry about it. Let it happen.

Surrender is to drop your argument with Life. See how this feels.

The Trick Of Suppression

"Something seeks to suppress emotions, to keep them stored and buried. Accept your emotions, let them be. From here they may either be outwardly expressed, or inwardly dissolved. Just watch what happens without expectation."

We all know that suppression is not helpful. It just builds up what hurts, to a point where it can become unhealthy, and you end up over-reacting to everything that happens.

That is a reason why the Painmaker can become so potent – years of suppression. Suppression is usually unconscious – we don't often choose to do it, it's rather that we don't know what else to do, and the Painmaker seeks to build up its reserves of life energy by suppressing emotions.

We can become so trained in what is the "right" way to feel, what is the "wrong" way to feel, how you "should or should not" feel in certain situations – that we can unconsciously bury the stuff that our conditioning labels as wrong or bad. Stop labeling anything, let the feelings be there if they wish.

Enjoying Suppression

Be aware that something often enjoys suppression, or storage of negative emotion. This is not the case for everyone, however. Often we can get caught in holding on to inner negativity and emotions, and continue to feed them internally. Something wants to hold on to them. You go to say something to express the feelings to another person, and then the suppression energy, which wishes to just keep the feelings alive inside, suppresses the expression. It throws up false inhibitions, fears of "maybe I just shouldn't say", or "what if I look stupid", or it analyses how effective saying something will be. This is a very clever trick. The reasons for non-expression are usually not true, they are just ways of making you hold on to negativity.

When you express emotion, it is somehow released, or exposed to be a ridiculous interpretation of reality – which is of course the greatest fear of the ego – it does not want to be exposed as foolish, it wants to pretend to be intelligent. The ego is the personal self which is built on concepts and opinions. If an opinion is expressed, then it is open to destruction, which the personal self feels it must avoid at all costs. It actually finds far greater safety in keeping negative thoughts inside, so it can hold on to them. Simply no longer be loyal to that which makes you suffer. Stop taking all this inner nonsense seriously.

When the negativity is held on to, it becomes like a dark cloud that is unconsciously cherished. When you find yourself complaining or criticising someone or something internally, you are creating suffering primarily for yourself. To be more accurate, the Painmaker is creating suffering. It loves to cling to negativity.

If suppression takes place, if negativity is being held on to inside, all you can do is watch it, accept it. Even suppression can become a habit, something that happens by itself, so your role is only to watch it happen, without trying to change it. This kind of clean observance exposes and dissolves what is negative and futile. It may not all happen at once, but when you watch and allow the habit of suppression, you see that it is not who you are.

This is not to say that you must always express yourself or speak your feelings. No. There are no rules. This is just to say how suppression of emotions, which is harmful to your inner state, can go on unnoticed, and how to resolve this. Don't be so concerned about how often you can "say something" – this is just more ego. Just no longer cling to negativity. If you are not resisting your emotions or the play of outer Life, words emerge if necessary, but it is no longer so personal. Nonresistance to Life means there is no longer a separation between "you" and Life. The inner person that clings to emotions and keeps them alive through stories, becomes dissolved.

We often get internally stuck because we give such belief and importance to our thoughts and emotions. We really believe that whatever the mind thinks, is true. Of course, it is not true. Thoughts and emotions can be there, but do not take them so seriously. Do not assume that they are representatives of truth. When you take each thought and emotion to be the truth of things, you naturally become enslaved. Then when the mind is resisting and judging Life, you feel as if the truth is not coming to fruition, that things should not be this way. This is suffering.

Expression

Expression of emotion need not be confrontational. If it appears that the actions of another have upset you, saying "when you do this, I feel a huge amount of anger inside" may be more beneficial than being completely taken over by the anger and saying "STOP DOING THAT YOU IDIOT!" - but again, it may depend on the situation! We always rob ourselves of intelligence when we plan what we will say, when we approach things with a pre-conceived idea of how is best to handle things. Just be open and empty, you will find actions and words emerging spontaneously without personal effort. Simply relax, even in the midst of tension. Be comfortable with being uncomfortable, then action will flow if needed. Don't be so responsible for yourself, don't police yourself. This does not mean you will be reckless, it means you will be free. Recklessness or what we call "childish irresponsibility" comes from inner claustrophobia, a lack of presence or a sense of discontentment. From freedom, when you are not judging yourself or policing your own actions, there is a background of peace, and so of course actions and words take on a finer quality from here, if they even emerge at all.

Surrender digs up the root of painful emotion, expression trims the branches. Don't get stuck doing neither.

If the emotion involves others, and you feel to say something but feel too afraid, notice how neither speaking to someone nor surrendering internally - is totally futile. Watch this tendency. To maintain the inner dialogue for no other purpose than to prolong suffering is insane. Notice the suffering it creates. From here you are more aware, more present, and if you relax, you will either find yourself taking direct action to express the emotion, or you will notice it dissolving inside yourself. You will not be so easily caught up in the "should I say something or not" pointless monologue. With nonresistance, you say what is needed if the moment requires. The moment speaks for you - you don't have to decide or "be brave" - it is no longer so personal. Be aware that any frustration of "not being able to say anything" is also part of the Painmaker. Surrender to this as well.

"I can never say how I feel" is only painful for us when we resist it, when we label it as bad, as if it should be different. If you fully accept it as if you had chosen it, then not only does this dissolve the self-inflicted suffering, it dissolves the tendency itself. All of these tendencies are part of the human condition in prolonging the existence of negative energies. It is nothing personal, so give your feelings space to be, allow yourself to feel whatever you feel without regret or criticism. This is self-forgiveness, which is not weakness as the mind will claim. It is strength and sanity. *Be* with what *is*, and see what happens.

We often become so trained in the importance of "being yourself" and of "saying how you feel", then if inhibitions arise when there is an impulse to say something, we can get into a mess of self-criticism and self analysis: "why can't I just say how I feel!". If you can't say how you feel, accept it. There is no problem. Often these "feelings" can be old reactions in disguise anyway, if they cause you pain, they are not true. Don't have an allegiance to what creates suffering. When you accept your feelings as well as your inhibitions, they lose their power. Whatever you internally fight or analyse internally just gets stronger, it gets more of your belief and interest, which keeps it alive.

Alleviation Of Suffering Is Primary, Action Is Secondary

Our main focus is the alleviation of suffering. For this, inner nonresistance is key, to what is happening inside and outside. When you let both the inner and outer be as they are, you naturally become aware of the truest aspect of yourself which is unaffected by both, which is not touched by what happens. But when you go out and control things or label things as yourself, there is a far stronger energetic connection between "you" and "things". This creates the illusion that you are very much involved in everything that happens, when in fact you are the space in which things happen. This is the space of true intelligence and creativity, which is not personal, and is the source of all useful action.

Don't Have An Ideal Self

"Chasing the idea of being a particular sort of person is futile. Simply accept yourself as you are, including all so-called flaws. This acceptance will dissolve what is useless, and allow your best traits to emerge and be of service."

One of our behaviours that appears to be beneficial for us, but actually ruins us internally, is "trying to be a certain way". For example if a person sees someone they admire, often the personal mind which seeks perfection (since it feels imperfect and incomplete) says "I want to be like that". The behaviour or character trait could be anything from kind, calm, honest, hard-working, confident, "enlightened", or anything else.

So the mind sets out on its mission to be a certain way. It can even create an ideal picture of "how I want to be", and it lists how it should be, which is surely "better" than how it is now. This may in fact be beneficial for some people. If it works for you, if you are happier because of it, great, stick with it if you feel to. But for many of us, it becomes exhausting and creates a kind of inner torture. The natural tendencies of the mind and body do not match up to the "ideal picture" that the mind is striving for, and all sorts of self-harming behaviours begin to emerge. Self-condemnation and self-criticism arise, which are utterly useless. Critical thoughts such as "why can't I be like 'this'", or "why can't I be like 'that'", "why can't I be confident" or "why can't I be more honest" can emerge – and then a circle of suffering ensues.

You will notice that with most "admirable characters" – they accept themselves for who they are. They are not trying to be like anyone else, they are simply being as they are, without trying to be better or different. They do not believe that they should be different in any way. Even if they have so-called "flaws" (which are just labels created by society), they accept it. They are not obsessed with trying to change themselves or trying to be "better". As a result they enjoy Life. Their allowance of self promotes ease, the sense of strain or neediness diminishes, and so the natural beneficial character traits (which are actually unique in every individual body) can come into fruition, and serve Life harmoniously.

An example is if we look at the great sages over history. At the essential level, they are all one, they share the same identity of awareness, but in their human expression, they all differ. They have different abilities, different ways of speaking, different habits in daily life, different occupations etc. No two humans are the same in their surface expression. What a miracle this is! But when our conditioning comes in, the needy human mind which creates our society ignores the miraculous uniqueness of each human in their expression, and instead holds up a sign that says "BE LIKE THIS".

Discard any idea you have about being any particular way. Discard all of your opinions and ideas about who you are. You need no identity or opinions of self to function effectively in the world. All of the ideas about yourself actually draw attention away from the natural peace within, beneath the resistance and ideas of "me".

We are so obsessed with the ideas of self-improvement or personal growth, that we miss the joy of being oneself – both one's true self, beyond birth and death, and also the joy of expressing in the world naturally, without judgements.

Whatever limiting or undesirable tendency or character trait you think you have, is usually based on a form of resistance. To resist it strengthens it, to accept it without judgement, burns its resistive foundation.

To accept your character traits and behaviours as they are, means you can become aware of the deeper aspect of yourself. The stillness, the *being* within which is not personal, and is not affected by the world, thoughts or emotions. Be finished with ideas of self-improvement. Your real Self needs no improvement. Be as you are. All useful action can arise spontaneously from here.

Dissolving Boredom

"Boredom can feel valid and justified, but it is simply the mind craving external stimulation. Sit with it, be with the feeling, allow it to be, and it cannot remain for long."

Boredom is a state of dissatisfaction or restlessness. No doubt it is not pleasant. The mind is so used to being fed from the outside with anything noisy, that when the noise is not there, it becomes disturbed. In the same way that a drug addict feels troubled when the drugs are removed, the mind can not stand external stimuli (on which it feels dependent) being taken away. The mind always wants stimulation. Without stimulation your thoughts would subside, so the mind-made identity would subside – and this is what the mind fears most. So, it will make you feel bored so that you give it stimulation and do not question its reality.

So how do dissolve boredom? You just stop running from it. Be with it. It will not last. Fully feel how boredom feels. You can even make it an investigation. Just be with the feelings without interpreting them, and without trying to get rid of them. When approached in this way, instantly their disturbing power is weakened. They are just sensations. Whatever you allow and accept fully cannot disturb you. You may notice at first that the feelings get worse, or your mind tries to distract itself with something to do, perhaps something totally insane or random. The mind may complain, resist, imagine things that are not here – let it all happen. Give up the fight. Just remain, relax for a moment, be an empty space for these feelings.

The boredom is then not such a big deal. It is just a feeling, which does not last. Beneath the feelings of boredom there is an impersonal, untouched space, a stillness without which no feeling could exist. Pay attention to this stillness, how it is at peace, how it needs nothing. In what way are you separate from this stillness? The only apparent separation is when you take yourself to be the thought of "I". What if you do not assume yourself to be any thought? Who are you then?

To get rid of boredom you can give the mind what it wants in some external stimuli – but then you are always its slave. Or you face boredom square on, without fearing it or suffering it. This removes boredom at the root, so it dissolves and does not return so easily.

The Cheat Of Jealousy

"One of the most useless emotions is jealousy. It is absolutely useless, and only serves to keep you feeling negative and separate from everyone else. In addition to this, it alters your energy field to be more repellant rather than attractive, which diminishes your own life experience's ability to enrich itself."

One of the most dishonest emotions is jealousy. What purpose does this thing even claim to serve?

The logic behind jealousy is this: *"someone else has something I want. Therefore I must feel jealous. Jealousy will destroy the other person, or at least take what they have away from them. Then I can have it, and then I will be happy because I will no longer feel jealous."*

Madness.

Believing in jealousy turns you into a repellant. You less easily attract anything positive or life-enhancing if you are carrying jealousy around. Notice how little it helps. It is totally destructive, and carries a foul smell. Again, you can notice that something, in a sick way, enjoys it. It makes the ego (the mind made self), seem more real. It enhances the idea of "me" and it strengthens the sense of separation between "me" and "another", which helps strengthen "me" even more.

Our society makes us believe in competition and scarcity. So we believe that if someone else has something, our chances of getting it are diminished. As if there is not enough to go around. This just isn't true. If you are happy for someone, welcoming their success or acquisition, you fill yourself with these same feelings of success or acquisition. If you feel jealous and wish someone didn't have something or achieve something, then you fill yourself with lack. Then you become respectively attractive or repellant. Truly what you do to others is what you do to yourself.

So when jealousy comes up, notice its futility, sense how it is enjoyed inside, or is believed to be useful. Then let it be. When you see that it no longer serves you, you will be able to let it go without any effort, in the same way that you would stop hitting yourself when you realise the act merely creates pain.

Undoing Loneliness

"It's beautiful to be alone. To be alone does not mean to be lonely. It means the mind is not influenced and contaminated by the society."

– Jiddu Krishnamurti

Loneliness is not something to be avoided anymore. Everyone has felt it to some extent. We can carry the fear of loneliness around through our entire experience of the world, but never face it and dissolve it. We always have a distraction, it may be the TV, it may be friends, it may be the spouse, it may be the Internet, or even work. Even the spiritual ideas of meditation can come in to mask the idea of loneliness, it fills the mind at least with an idea that it is doing something, some pre-occupation or perceived activity.

Simply face loneliness without trying to change it. You may be surprised at what happens when you no longer try to avoid it, when you no longer fear the feeling, when you can let it be there without interpreting it, without taking it personally. It is a feeling, perhaps attached to thoughts and a personal identity – that is all. It is not something you need to try to overcome or manage or do anything about. Do absolutely nothing about it. There is actually a huge power in doing absolutely nothing, in looking absolutely nowhere. Then you are being yourself, but of course the false self hates this, since it can no longer survive or be taken as real.

Loneliness is always based on the "me", the personal mind that feels unsatisfied, alone in the universe, separate from all things, disempowered, desperate for something to alleviate its background misery. Being alone exposes this fully. The mind can no longer be distracted, its discontent can no longer be masked or suppressed. It is fully here, and it is not pleasant.

All of its fears and insecurities are at the surface, trying to create trouble. "Just do something, watch TV..." all of these impulses are to alleviate the mind from its own burden. Don't run any more. Let it be there. It does not last when you give up your aversion to loneliness, when you no longer wish it were different. Simply experience it as it is, without analysing or telling a story about it. This is the way to treat everything, allow it, let the experience be as it is.

Perhaps it is programmed in us somewhere to resist being alone, to always seek advice and further programming from external sources. As Krishnamurti said, in aloneness the mind is no longer contaminated by society. We are always taught to get our answers from someone else, to look outside for our solutions. Rarely are we told to turn within, to live from an inner truth rather than a prescribed set of ideals from someone else. Rebel. Be alone and fully embrace what is felt. All of the inner turmoil becomes burnt in this inner environment. It may not be comfortable at first, but just give up the idea of "trying to get somewhere else", set aside the need for things to be different in how you feel, give up the argument.

As it is seen that this personal self, the inner commentator, is merely a creation of thought, that the individual self is a mere appearance in the ocean of being, or consciousness, then who is left to be lonely? Loneliness begins to lose its meaning, since in a sense, you are the only one here, you are the one consciousness that gives rise to all things.

No Worries

"Worry. A most cherished yet most limiting behaviour.

You are not the worrier, the worrier arises in you."

We always get taught the value of worry. Everyone is worried about something, concerned in some way, and so we pick it up. You may notice that there always seems to be something to be worried about, some burden to carry. This is not to do with the outer world, it is an addiction of the mind.

We often believe we have to worry about stuff, that worry is perfectly normal and justified, even part of being a responsible and sane individual. Let's question this. If worry is valid as a behaviour, then it must serve us in some way, it must be helpful to our life situations. So what useful purpose does worrying serve?

Either you see that it serves absolutely no useful purpose, or you think it helps get things done. Fear is often a motivating force for many people's actions, and worry can be part of this motivator. But this is a trick. You do not need worry in order to act in the world. You can still lock your doors at night without worrying and imagining what might happen. You can still care for someone without worrying about them.

Worrying is such a supreme waste of energy, that is of no service to you or the world. Then the mind says "but I can't help worrying, it's part of who I am, it's part of being a mother, a father, a friend, a sibling, or it's part of being effective at what I do". The mind becomes dependent on worrying, since its identity now rests on it. You would likely be far more effective in whatever role you have if you were not burdened with worry. The mind loves to worry and it will say anything to make you believe it is justified.

If you want to worry, no one can stop you. If you wish to be free from worry, simply recognise that the "worrier", or the "worry energy" arises *in* you. You yourself are not the worrier. Worry arises by itself. All-consuming thoughts of negativity, imagined possibilities, a sense of helplessness - all go round in circles and consume the mind. Be aware that this is happening, and laugh at the madness of it all. Whether you are worrying about yourself or another, see that the worry creates a cherished object (a thought of yourself or a thought of someone else) and then places that cherished object in negative circumstances. How is this helpful? If anything, it is destructive and insane. You can also be aware that all identities involved in the worry are only creations of thought. Whether it is you or other people - they are *only thoughts* of you or other people, they are not true representatives of anyone. These identities are merely creations of the mind placed in imaginary circumstances.

If worrying is happening, let it. You can not argue or analyse - this just makes worry worse. Let it be there, but no longer give your interest to contributing to such a destructive and harmful energy. It really does not help. If you can see this for yourself, it will naturally drop off, and you will be aware of the lightness that can emerge when you are no longer carrying useless burdens.

Part 2

How To's

When I first began writing the website www.InnerPeaceNow.com, I wrote the specifics of how to deal with certain troubling emotions, as they came to me at the time. Some of these are in this eBook, and have often been expanded on.

The basic premise is always the same – emotions are not who you are, allow, accept, do not take seriously, do not judge, be the space for them. The following articles go into more detail for those who would like...

How To Stop Being Concerned About Other People's Opinions

"If you take your own opinions and self-judgements seriously, you are bound to take other people's opinions and judgements seriously as well. If your opinions and ideas about yourself fall away, if you can be here without needing to imagine yourself to be someone or something, then where is the harm in judgements or opinions from others?

The judgements we fear from others are merely the judgements we have about ourselves that we do not like."

It all comes down to your own mind. We are so trained to believe in the concept of "other people", to believe in separateness, that it can feel very real in the mind. Other people exist for us mainly as thoughts. For example, a family member. It is likely that when you think about them, you get a certain feeling, along with a mental image and a name. This is all imagination. It is the mind's interpretation of another being. Names are just labels, thoughts are just thoughts. To see someone as they really are means to not add labels to them, to not add opinions and thoughts onto who the mind thinks they are. Then they are seen as they really are – nameless, pure being, perhaps with an overlay of ego or personal mind – but this is sensed energetically rather than it being an interpretation that sticks inside you.

If you withdraw your judgements of others, then other people are on your mind less, since they no longer exist for you as concepts. If someone else does not exist for you as a concept, then the idea of them (which is purely a mental creation) can not plague the mind. Most of us think about "what he or she thought of me", question "what will they think of me?", or perhaps "what do they think of me now?" – but all of this is pure imagination, fictional identities created by the mind.

Even the "me" that fears being judged is just another thought that is believed in.

If you give up having opinions about other people, if you are less judgmental, or at least give less importance to your mind's judgements, then the importance of judgements from "others" about "you" will similarly fall away.

If you really value the mind's opinions about who you are, the mental labels that it has assigned itself over time, then naturally you will value the opinions of others just as much. The only reason the mind fears the judgement of others, is that it fears its own judgements being exposed, and the personal self being diminished as a result.

Let's take a common insecurity, such as someone believing they look too old. One human being carries no opinion of themselves, cares not how the body appears to others. The other person believes that the body is who they are, believes that it looks old, and for some reason hates this. Someone then approaches the first person, and begins to laugh at how old they look. "You look so old it's ridiculous" - this doesn't mean anything to the first person. There is no person inside the body that holds an opinion of "me looking old", and there is no-one inside who cares either way. So the inner state is untroubled. When this happens to the second person, however, there is trouble. A huge reaction flares up in the body, resistance, embarrassment, shame - all sorts of things. The opinion is being held "I look old and this is bad", and so when the same opinion seems to come from outside, it charges the latent negativity in the person to come to the surface. The negativity is fully felt as if it were true. Perhaps counter-opinions or self-justifications arise to combat the negative opinion - "I don't look *that* old!" - in an attempt to suppress the negative opinion and identity, more opinions come to fight it. Instead of fighting, if the person were to let their opinions of themselves come to the surface and naturally be seen as *only thoughts* - then this experience is a therapeutic one – the outer criticism shows the negativity they are clinging to, perhaps without even knowing. The outside voices just highlight the inner ones, the ones that may escape the radar.

Whatever judgements you fear from other people simply show you what you still believe, and do not like about yourself. That is all. It is no more than that. The mind does not want its imagined flaws to be confirmed. It wants to pretend it is strong and indestructible, rather than weak and shaky – which of course it is, since it is not real.

It all starts with you. If you are less judgmental of other people and yourself, the judgements or potential judgements of others become far less potent. If you take your own opinions less seriously, you will naturally take the opinions of others less seriously. You feel less of a need to protect any idea or image of yourself or your life. If you realise that all of your opinions and ideas about who you are, what's good about you, what's bad about you, what you are doing right and what you are doing wrong – if you can see that these are all merely ideas, subject to change, extremely unstable, not to be taken seriously – then you can see this in other's opinions as well.

As the sage Nisargadatta Maharaj, in response to praise, said: "Your high opinion of me is your opinion only. Any moment you may change it. Why attach importance to opinions, even your own?".

Opinions are so transient, so fleeting, so unstable. Yet our belief in them makes them seem very solid and real. We are trained to believe that praise means we are good and criticism means we are bad. We are taught there is value in being perceived highly, and shame in being perceived badly. All of this is nonsense.

We attach our Self to so many opinions – "I am this, I am that, I am so and so". The truth is you *are*, all else is false conditioning. You feel you *are*, that you exist, that you are alive, and then the parents and teachers basically say: "this feeling of existence that you are aware of, is directly linked to and dependent on this fragile and transient body. You are this body!" And so the fear of death, along with great psychological personal suffering ensues.

Simply relax from judging yourself and others. If you have no opinion of yourself, how can the opinions of others affect you? It is all meaningless. No matter what opinion anyone has of you, no matter what is said, does it actually affect who you are in truth? You are awareness – can awareness be affected by anything in it, including opinions of self? A remark by another may destroy your surface identity, you feel diminished as a person, but what knows this? What is aware of this person's feelings being hurt? Does this awareness care for any opinion? Do opinions affect it, or is it naturally and effortlessly beyond the judgements of the human mind?

Whenever anyone claims to have an opinion of you, it is not really about you. It is about them. Their opinion is a creation of their own mind, based on a bundle of thoughts that they call "you". Do you see the illusion of it all? The same goes for your opinions about other people – it is all a creation of one personal mind, trying to understand things that cannot be understood through concepts. Everyone's opinions about you are only reflections of their own minds. They are not really to do with you at all. That's why some people may think highly of you, and others may not. Fully accept that no one has to like you or think well of you. Be fully with the feelings or the fears of not being liked, or of being judged a certain way, be with the feelings, accept them as they are, and they will no longer dominate you.

As the spiritual teacher Gangaji has said:

"People will judge, it is the nature of mind activity.

Let yourself feel totally judged insane, absurd, stupid, whatever it is you imagine that would be so hard to bear, invite it.

You will see that it is nothing, simply judgment.

As long as you fear judgment, there is a sensed lack of freedom to be who you are.

Be finished with the prison of others' opinions."

There is nothing wrong with opinions, but when they are believed to be the truth of things, and when the identity becomes attached to them, we suffer.

Drop the belief in good and bad judgements. Someone's judgement of you, or your judgement of yourself is not what does most harm. Trouble comes when you believe the judgement is either good or bad. Then the "good" judgements inflate the ego, making it feel less of a burden. This is a pleasant feeling. We can become attached to this pleasure, and so habitually seek approval or acceptance from others. The "bad" judgements are then seen to be painful, since the ego resists and contracts, and so we believe that being judged negatively by others is something to avoid. See things as they are. Drop the labels of good and bad, just to see how it feels.

The Being Prior To Opinions

Your real being is the simple sense of existence, the feeling "I AM". It can first be felt when you take your attention inwards, just to feel your own presence. How does it feel to simply *be*, to be here, without needing to be elsewhere? What is important is how it *feels*. This natural feeling of existence is your true Self, all the other ideas of "I am this" and "I am that", are merely ideas, mostly brought about through conditioning of society, parents, teachers etc. The true essence can only be felt, the feeling that you are alive, awake, existent. Let this feeling be the background of your life – to be felt as the foundation of your experience. Without you, nothing else would appear. Your existence is the source of everything else being experienced. Pay attention to yourself as this being, which is one with silence, or space, or existence itself. You then notice that out of this being comes the dance of Life - the outer forms and the inner forms all rise and fall in this ocean of being. This sense of *being* is not limited to one body, it is within all bodies, all objects, it is the one, impersonal consciousness, in which the imagined personal self temporarily arises. It is beyond opinions and ideas - prior to them, without which no opinion could exist.

How To Deal With Anxiety

"Anxiety is just an energy of resistance. It is trapped Life energy. Allow it. Do not try to change it. Do not take it personally. It is just another aspect of the Painmaker. When you no longer fight it or take it to be who you are, you are free, and its strength weakens by itself."

Awareness and acceptance of anxiety transmute it into inner peace.

- When you are aware of anxiety, there is a separation between you and the emotion.

- When you accept anxiety, the resistive energy of it can not survive for long.

Resistance Is Futile

Whether you go through periods of extreme anxiety or you just find yourself feeling a bit nervous from time to time, deal with anxiety in the same way.

Let it be. Know that it is ok to feel these feelings. Completely accept that they are there. Do not resist them or try to think your way out of them. When you completely accept feelings like this, straight away they become less unbearable. So many of our problems with anxiety come from a resistance to it, thinking about how we do not like the feelings, how we want the feelings to go away, or how they are "wrong". If you let the feelings *be*, much of the pain you have identified with separates from you.

Instead of resisting the discomfort of anxiety, see what happens if you fully surrender to it, what happens if you completely allow it to *be*, without objection?

From this point the anxiety energy may still be inside you,

even taking over your thoughts completely. Know that you are the *awareness* behind the emotion, the *awareness* behind the anxious thoughts. These thoughts and emotions are not who you are at all. You are that which simply knows they are there. You are the space in which these thoughts and emotions play out, so just be the space for them. Give no sense of self to them, even though the thoughts say "I".

When you can observe anxiety as a certain energy within your field of awareness, you are not part of it any more. You no longer say "I am anxious" or "I am nervous", but rather feel that there is this certain energy within you. This is disidentification from emotion, which removes its power. Do not force the energy/emotion away, just feel it, observe it, be the space for it, and it weakens all by itself.

I can not stress enough the power of acceptance over any negative emotional state. When you completely accept it as it is and do not even desire to change it, it miraculously changes all by itself. It either subsides or may remain for a while longer – yet in this state of acceptance you are free in either case.

Anxiety is a form of resistance. Your nonresistance to it means that this resistance can not take you over, and can not survive for long.

When you feel anxious – know that there is something in you that is enjoying it – this is the Painmaker. The purpose of your anxiety is to feed the Painmaker and keep the ego in place.

Imagining "The Future"

Anxiety is some form of negative anticipation of the future. "The future" seems to be so real in your mind – but have you ever noticed how "the future" is just part of your imagination that you call "the future"? Have you also noticed that all of these future thoughts are actually made up of past thoughts?

The ego is conditioned by the past and then projects these past thoughts into "future" circumstances – but it is all just an illusion.

Do not give the voice of anxiety any authority. All it does is cause you pain. Do not resist it, just let it *be*. Just letting it *be* implies it has no authority over you, and that it is not a threat. In the same way you may see a bird flying across the sky in the distance, just observe your anxiety without trying to interfere with it.

How to deal with anxiety actually requires no effort. It is more of a relinquishment of effort to change it, and through this you are aware of yourself, as awareness.

Anxiety may still seem very strong, but just remain *as* the present moment. Accepting the present moment fully includes all the thoughts and emotions that are within it. Relinquish any belief in controlling your thoughts and emotions. When you surrender and give up your need to control, you actually gain control through transcending what *is*.

We like to believe that we should be able to stop feeling anything unpleasant through some sort of resistance or interference with our emotions. Strangely, interfering does the opposite – it gives our thoughts and emotions strength. Surrender takes their authority and power away.

It Isn't Personal

Anxiety claims to be extremely personal. The mind forms a conceptual identity (the self-image), and basis anxiety on this image of a person. This *mental concept* of who you are is only another thought. It is a conditioned identity. When anxiety arises, the anxious self has a strong aversion to its own anxiety. It wants the anxiety to be gone, and undergoes great suffering. If we can surrender this personal will, give up the belief that we have the power to change it, then suddenly we become aware of a deeper, impersonal power beneath the anxiety, that is naturally at peace. Who you are is the awareness in which this anxious self arises.

Notice that anxiety truly has a mind of its own. It comes unannounced, with no choice on your part. It charges thoughts with its own energy. Watch it without judgement. Then you naturally see that it is not who you are, and its grip is weakened without effort.

The Purpose

Anxiety claims to be helpful. It claims to be some kind of defense mechanism. But what is it defending? What is being protected? "Me", or "I" is being protected – but what is this "me" or "I" – is it nothing more than a thought? If social anxiety is in you, enquire – does the body fear its own destruction in a social interaction? Likely not. Do you fear the body being destroyed by social interaction? Likely not. So what feels threatened? Only the illusory, personal self. The ghost in the head. Anxiety is the attempted defence of an illusion, and yet serves no useful purpose. To see the futility of anxiety is to end your relationship with it.

The Unaffected Awareness

If anxiety is there, you know. If anxiety is not there, you know. You are here when anxiety is acting out or not. Anxiety comes to visit. It creates "an anxious person". You are also aware of this anxious person, so how could it be who you are?

If you wish anxiety to be gone, it stays. If you welcome it and be with it, it dissolves.

Be aware that whatever is happening, you are aware of it. A calm mind, a frantic mind, ease or anxiety – all arise and fall

IN you. You are the awareness in which these things play. Be aware of yourself as this. The awareness is not personal, it does not suffer what arises, it simply remains as neutral, empty awareness.

Forget What You Know

Forget what you have been told about anxiety. We get so conditioned into thinking it is wrong, bad or undesirable, that when it shows up we resist it and make it even stronger. It is an energy field that cannot stand you being with it nonjudgementally. It needs you to hate it, it needs you to feel troubled by it.

When you know that this anxiety is just the Painmaker acting out - you can disidentify from it. Do not take it so seriously. Smile at the insanity of it all, completely imagining things yet claiming that it is all so real. Observe and accept, that is all you need to do.

How To Deal With Conflict

"Conflict is mainly in our reactions to situations, rather than the situations themselves. Be aware of how the mind is quick to judge situations, and that what causes us most harm, is this reaction."

The main thing is to stop believing what the inner man or woman says about conflict. This inner man or woman in the body is no different from the ego, or the personal self. We are often so conditioned in imagining conflict when there is none, that a simple conversation can become an object of fear or discomfort.

Quality of action is always relative to our inner state. If we are full of fear and resistance, these are not necessarily bad things, but the outer actions will reflect these inner energies. We simply have to relinquish the ideas we have about ourselves and situations, and allow action to spontaneously and impersonally emerge. It's quite simple when we realise that our conditioning in certain areas of life only creates suffering and unnecessary drama.

Conflict is a big favourite for the personal self, it loves conflict, loves trouble, loves disturbance. If you had no conflict between the inner and outer reality of your life, then who would you be?

Arguments

People usually argue because of the personal self in them. This personal self identifies with a mental position or conceptual identity, and when this is threatened, the entire false sense of self becomes threatened. If this mental position or concept is destroyed, then so is part of the personal self – and this is what it fears most...

This is where anger and negative emotions arise from during

arguments – they are usually egoic defence mechanisms.

You may have noticed by now that once the discussion escalates into an argument, both (or all) parties become taken over by emotion and defensiveness, and get nowhere.

Less progress is made the more the argument strengthens. People lose their sense of logic or reasoning because they feel their sense of selves are on the line – which they see as more important than actually resolving a situation.

Sometimes arguments are completely pointless. There may be nothing that even needs to be done or resolved. The argument is just about an idea or concept.

Other times, of course, they arise due to someone's actions or behaviour that another person/s reacts negatively to.

Dealing With Arguments

So, how do you actually deal with them? Use arguments as spiritual practice – use them to dissolve your ego through becoming aware of what happens inside you during an argument.

Let the other person *be*. Watch them tie themselves up in a knot of anger and confusion. You can say what you need to, but you do not have to argue. You can accept that everyone has their own brain and is entitled to their own point of view – but you do not have to resist or react negatively.

When you are in this non-resistive state you do not harbour any negativity, and you can see things more clearly. If you need to take any action or say anything, it flows from a peaceful place within you.

Being able to see the difference between someone's egoic behaviour and who they actually are can help you to stay at peace.

Conflict implies two things going against each other. If you remain at peace while another argues, then how can this be conflict?

We often get into arguments when we take other people too seriously. If someone is saying some nonsense, rather than seeing it as nonsense, as untruth expressing itself, the untrue aspect of ourselves "buys" it as serious, and a whole big thing ensues. We take other people seriously when we take ourselves seriously. We are always brought up to be very protective of our personal selves, believing we are serious and should be taken seriously. Drop it for a moment. Look around, look at the sky. The body that you are aware of is an infinitesimally small yet intricate part of this vast universe.

We tend to look at smaller creatures such as ants and see them as tiny, and in our arrogance we usually see smaller creatures as quite insignificant compared to us. Yet, if you are far above the ground looking down at the earth, humans are just like ants. Everything is relative. We all tend to think we are very important, imagining our lives to be very important, but are they? Do you realise how massive this manifest universe is? Do the details of our lives really matter? They do to the personal self. Everything in "my Life" matters to the personal self - everything is meaningful, clung to, and personal. This is because the permanent, valuable nature of our true being becomes confused and tied in with very fleeting and unstable forms. From the viewpoint of the impersonal being, all of this is a transient play, which is not so burdensome.

Spiritual Practice

You may notice feelings of anger, fear, defensiveness or even rage arising in you during an argument - this is a chance to bring in awareness, to free yourself from the shackles of your own egoic reactions.

What you are fearful or defensive of is likely based on concepts - your imagination.

Observe the reactions and emotions in yourself as if you are the space in which they arise. Notice how they arise all by themselves. This breaks identification with them. Acceptance of emotions dissolves them into deeper peace. Through this you become more in touch with what you really are.

If you get criticised or verbally abused - you may feel an uncomfortable feeling inside you - almost like part of you is dying. This is the imaginary personal self and its associated energies. Do absolutely nothing, let the diminishment happen. If you let it happen, you become aware of the truest aspect of yourself, beneath the idea of being a person. As the ego becomes destroyed (which it finds uncomfortable), you are aware of the impersonal Self - awareness - which can not be destroyed.

Let your ego take a bashing and realise what is still there even after your form identity or conceptual identity has been destroyed - you are still there, but free of thought forms. The awareness that you are cannot be harmed.

Personal selves love arguments because it makes them feel more alive and separate from other people. If you resist an argument, you strengthen it. So just let it be and see how your mind tries to trick you into labeling the situation as bad, or feeling any defensiveness or negativity - it is all an illusion.

Someone is just speaking (or shouting) - they are just noises coming out of someone's mouth, yet something inside you likes to react to all of this and take it all personally. See how funny this all is as it takes place inside you. Do not take your reactions (or anyone else's reactions) so seriously.

Feel the relief in no longer needing to defend your opinions or ideas. If people criticise, verbally attack or argue against you – know that you have nothing to defend – you can not be harmed. What is there to defend in conversations? Just ideas and opinions, not who you are. You still say what may be required, but it is no big deal.

From this state you become free of other people's drama, and situations of conflict become far easier to deal with – whether they are physical or not.

Do Not Suppress!

There is a difference between suppressing and accepting your emotions during conflict. If you suppress your emotions by thinking you should not be feeling them or in any way resisting them, this just makes your pain worse. Do not confuse this suppression of emotion with complete acceptance.

If there is no peace, this means there is no acceptance. When you accept your feelings, you stop trying to change them or force them away. If you are suppressing them, you are still identified with the emotions and there is no sense of spaciousness or acceptance.

Of course you can always express the negative emotions if you wish, this is much better than leaving unresolved negativity within you.

Conflict Is In Your Reaction

Conflict may feel uncomfortable only if you interpret the situation in this way. Notice any feelings of unease arising within you, and transmute them in to peace through acceptance of their existence.

The ego does not know how to deal with conflict. It believes the only way to deal with conflict is through resistance.

It is your resistance to and reaction to "conflict" that makes it seem uncomfortable or undesirable, and tends to just make the situation worse. Separate the situation from your reaction to it or thoughts about it.

When you accept the situation as it is, you become one with it. This includes accepting any negative reactions within you. You then do not have to think about how to deal with conflict – action either arises or does not arise by itself.

Conflict is just a perception of reality, rather than the reality itself.

Indirect Conflict

You may experience feelings of conflict after the conflicting situation has passed, or if you are around a person you previously conflicted with. This is just the ego's way of holding on to the past so it can form some kind of identity. Notice how there is someone inside you that likes to feel hard done by, mistreated or in any way negative about something or someone else. This person also loves to blame and nurture animosity towards others.

As you notice this or any other uncomfortable thoughts, feelings or re-living of situations in your mind, smile at them. Be the space for them and see that they are only serving the purpose of keeping the personal self alive.

Physical Conflict

When you are surrendered to what the moment holds, you have no concepts in your mind that prevent you from taking right action. Then when a seemingly threatening situation arises such as being physically attacked, whatever needs to be done will happen without you even needing to think about it.

You will not ask how to deal with conflict, you will just act if necessary.

You will not be limited by thinking you shouldn't be violent because you are a "spiritual person". Right action will not be stopped by fear, nor will you feel like violence is necessary to uphold your false sense of self. You may use violence or you may not, but there will be some degree of freedom within you, and there will be far less malice or resistance behind any of your actions.

The main thing to focus on is your inner state. The exterior world (including the actions of your body) then take care of themselves. Be surrendered, welcoming what comes and letting your actions be moved from here.

Conflict In Your Own Mind

Of course everything is in your own mind. Even what you perceive to be other people is just an image in your mind. However conflict does not necessarily have to be between two individuals. You could experience much conflict within yourself about a number of things such as solutions to problems, what the right thing to do is, or how to be a certain way.

It may seem that the harder you try to deal with this conflict through thinking about it, the worse it gets.

Listen to what your mind is doing – are there two voices in your head? Are you more identified with one than the other? Do you believe one of these voices to be you? Do you think any of these thoughts are who you are?

You are not the thinker of thoughts, you are the *awareness* in which they arise. Some people I have met have a voice in their head they are aware of, and another voice that they believe is them, arguing with the first voice or trying to out-think the first voice.

None of the thoughts or "voices in the head" are who you are. Just listen to these voices without judging them. This does not mean you are crazy when I say "voices in the head" – everyone has them, as thoughts, but most people see it as completely normal, because they believe the voice is who they are. You are the space in which the voice can *be*, the consciousness that gives power to the thought by believing it is you.

Once you begin to just listen to what your thoughts do, you realise they arise by themselves, and that they are not part of who you are. Then you can become more aware of the spacious, still awareness, the source of "I" and its related thoughts – which is what you are. An inspired solution to any problem will then arise from here, from deeper within you, or you may realise that what you thought was a problem actually was completely created by the mind to keep it occupied, and that no solution is even necessary.

You may find yourself allowing things to *be* and to take their own way, rather than imposing yourself and your desires on to things.

Resisting What Already *Is*

You may also feel conflict in yourself through trying to "be somewhere else", wanting reality to be different from how it is now. You may want to be different, have a different life situation, possession, status, job, whatever. If you want these things, this is not what causes you most pain. What causes you most pain is resisting the present moment. If you resist it, you suffer. If you accept it, you are instantly at peace, and far more ready to take any useful action.

We tend to see it as normal for things to happen on "the outside", whilst on the "inside" there is a person who reacts, resists and judges what is happening. This very energy is the ego, the personal self, and is the original conflict that we all experience – the conflict with Life itself. It is possible to no longer separate yourself from Life and what is happening, by no longer offering resistance to what arises in your awareness. Although we are trained to think this is weakness, you may be surprised that you are then one with the very source of Life itself, which is naturally creative in its action.

Your mind may object and claim resistance is necessary for progress, but the only reason you believe in "progress" being good is so that eventually you can be more happy, at ease or peaceful. Really the only time for all that "fullness of life" is right now, beyond the physical form of reality.

When you are in a state of full acceptance, any action towards progress will be far more effective.

This acceptance is also very useful during conflict with another individual. Situations such as these then tend to resolve themselves much easier when you are not internally resisting them. Instead of wishing someone to be different, such as less angry or less hateful towards you, simply let them be as they are. Acceptance in these situations may seem difficult and illogical, yet they are times where acceptance has the most powerful and peaceful results.

Dealing with conflict is easier when you are one with the present moment. To be one with it, you must fully accept it. Then the present moment uses you for the benefit of all.

However, often action may not even be necessary. You may notice that what you used to perceive as conflict is not conflict at all, it was just your reaction that made you believe it was real.

How To Deal With Pain

"Be aware that pain, be it physical or emotional, arises in you, rather than you arising in it. Suffering is most potent when we believe or desire that the feelings should be different. To relinquish this belief or desire, and to instead want things to be as they are, is the most miraculous state of mind – it allows for healing, although it makes no sense to our conditioning."

Resisting Pain Makes It Worse

Whenever we feel any kind of pain – physical or emotional – we tend to reject it. We tend to try to get rid of it through internal resistance.

This resistance is the thing that really makes us suffer. We then become in conflict with the present moment. The pain is there, and we are resisting it. Resistance has no healing quality, it just makes pain worse.

Nonresistance

With pain comes the natural desire for it not to be there. Pain often carries with it, or at least provokes, an intense resistance. The resistance can develop into psychological anguish, with thoughts such as "this is awful. I'm in so much pain. Why is this here? Why can't this go away? Why is this happening?".

The resistance is what creates most suffering, but it can be so inextricably linked to pain, that it can go unnoticed. Be unnatural and simply no longer argue with pain. If it is there, to fight it makes it worse. Surrender your desire for the pain to be gone. The desire for the pain to be gone is what makes you suffer most. No longer wish it be different. If resistance is still there, let this be there as well, no longer wish or expect things to be otherwise, and allow fully. See what happens.

The human mind believes that resisting the pain will diminish it and make it leave. Resistance hardens pain and intensifies suffering. Resistance to pain does the opposite of what it claims to do. It actually only maintains suffering and the sense of separate identity.

Without resistance to pain, it is easier to notice the untouched space in which the sensation arises. The space is not personal, and does not suffer...

Attention

Pain often consumes the attention at first. It can seem as if there is only the pain. Attention combined with resistance fuels the pain, so as well as nonresistance, we can notice that pain arises in a space of no-pain. In the same way that a cloud exists due to the sky, pain exists in the space of being, or the space of consciousness. Notice that this emptiness surrounding pain is not involved or affected by pain. It is not personal. The pain and the person affected by the pain arise in this space. You are neither the pain nor the person affected by the pain (which is only a self-image). Be the space for it. Nonresistance helps with this.

If helpful, the breath is always a useful tool to redirect attention from pain or its related resistance.

Who Is Suffering?

Who is suffering this? The worst part of pain is the "me" that suffers the pain. This can be particularly acute with things such as headaches, since the "me" that suffers it is often felt to be in the head – right where the pain is. The inner person that suffers pain is also observed by you. Locate the one who is suffering. Is the sufferer a real entity? Can he or she be found? Is it in fact just another thought or energy that arises in you, that previously was given huge belief and importance?

Another way of approaching this is to say – as you look inwardly – when pain is there, does the body suffer? Does the body wish the pain were gone? You may find that the body in itself is not the personal sufferer of pain. So does consciousness suffer? Consciousness is not a person that can suffer – pure consciousness is not personal. It is more like a space that allows the content to be as it is – so it is not the consciousness that suffers. So who is suffering? The idea of yourself suffers, and when involved with pain, the self-image becomes the very embodiment of suffering. Seeing that the one suffering is not real – but only an idea in the mind – will allow it to dissolve.

The self-image, or the ego, is the inner person who suffers pain. It feels as if it is literally *in* the pain – "I'm in pain!". It has a natural aversion to pain, it always wants pain to be gone, and in this wanting pain to be gone, it creates immense suffering. It uses pain as an excuse to really turn up the resistance, which it survives on. The key is to give up this fight, and no longer wish pain to be gone. This reverses suffering.

Investigating The Reality Of Pain

Once the pain has become less unbearable using the above guidelines, you may wish to investigate the pain – what is it really? If you drop all name-calling and assumptions about what pain is and what it means – then what is it? Can it actually be defined or located? Can you find a point where it starts and stops? What is pain made of? As you go into the pain directly, in a surrendered, non-resistive state, you may find the apparent solidity and "realness" of pain dissolves somewhat.

Pain often commands great belief, respect and importance. To simply not believe in pain, to not take it to be real, at least can remove its forceful pulling power over your attention.

Try this experiment: When pain arises in you, welcome it as if it is pleasure. Stop calling it pain, do not identify with it, and feel it fully as if it is enjoyable.

This may seem strange, but it is a very transcendent technique.

Does awareness change? Pain and pleasure come and go. The awareness that knows this – does it suffer what arises in it? Does it not remain as it is, impersonal, unaffected in its essence? Be aware that you are this awareness, which has no location or objective existence.

Don't identify with pain. Don't call it "mine". Don't even call it "pain". Our attempts to solve the pain through resisting it are quite futile. Go the other way, give up, let it be there.

How To Deal With Pain In Others

Again, acceptance is the key. We are always taught to resist pain in any form, whether it is our own or another's, but resistance itself is a form of pain, so how can it really help us? Acceptance of someone else's pain does not mean you are less likely to help. It actually means that there is more likely to be a solution that arises if one is possible.

If you resist someone's pain, you are helping to strengthen the collective pain energy. Acceptance of pain transmutes it into greater peace, and promotes a healing, intelligent environment, inwardly and outwardly.

How To Deal With Depression

"Be aware of it, feel it, notice its addictive quality, notice its futility, fully allow it without wanting it to leave. Fully embrace."

Often we believe that in order to deal with depression, we must change something externally, distract ourselves or analyse what we think is causing us to be depressed. There is nothing wrong with making external changes, but the quickest and most useful answer to how to deal with depression is to use the suffering to become more conscious and fully aware of what you are.

If you transcend the depression at this moment, you will be at peace and able to take any useful action if necessary. If no action can be taken, you will still be at peace - perhaps even more at peace - since there is nothing else you can do.

Depression can be useful to force you out of identification with any false sense of self, so that you can experience deeper inner peace and freedom.

If used correctly, depression is a teacher that burns up the illusions of yourself and takes you deeper into your true reality.

The Power Of Acceptance

How would you feel if you totally and completely accepted your current emotional state? If you are depressed, completely allow the feeling of depression to be there. Do not try to change it or break free from it, just completely accept the emotions as if you have chosen that they be there.

Instant acceptance is one of the most powerful answers to depression.

Really allow this now, as an experiment. What happens to your sense of depression or suffering when you totally accept and allow your feelings to *be?*

When you accept your depression as if you have chosen to feel this way, suddenly there is a new energy that arises in you. You are no longer resisting and feeding the depression, but transmuting it into greater peace through your radical acceptance. Depression can not survive for long in a space of embracing acceptance.

Take the attitude of "I will no longer suffer. Therefore, I welcome and accept all that arises within me." Stay in this state, do not get sucked back into identification with resistance, do not believe that you are the depression itself.

You Are Not The Depression

There is no need to identify with it.

The feelings of depression are just emotions that have been invested with a sense of self, a sense of "I". This is what gives them power. To remove this identification and remove their power, feel yourself as the *awareness* of the depression, and simply accept what arises.

As soon you experience yourself as *awareness* of the depression, you are no longer so connected to the emotion. The depression may not suddenly dissolve, and may still carry a sense of "I", but simply remain as the pure awareness of it. The depression is arising within the space of awareness that you are, but it is not you. Remain as the awareness that does not judge or resist what arises within it.

Then accept what arises completely. Do not give your power away to these painful emotions and thoughts. Let them *be*, and remain as the space, the stillness that is untouched by pain, suffering or depression.

Amongst the changing emotions and thoughts that you experience, there is a stillness that is unchanged and unaffected. It can be perceived as the nothingness or emptiness surrounding thoughts and emotions. Give your attention to this unchanging space, rather than the changing things that arise within it.

Notice that this silent space is not personal, it remains unchanged and unmoved despite the unhappy feelings and the unhappy person that may be arising within it. Remain as this untouched, untroubled space.

The moment you accept your feelings, you will no longer suffer. They will then disappear by themselves, as you are no longer feeding them through resistance and identification.

Do not decide whether or not the emotions should be present. Stop resisting or upsetting yourself that depression is there. The moment you totally accept your inner state, you will be free, whether depression is still there or not.

Don't Believe The Mind

Your mind may give you plenty of reasons and stories that seem to justify being depressed, sad or unhappy. Do not believe in these thoughts. As they arise, let them be, but do not give yourself to them. They arise and disappear by themselves, whilst you are constantly aware in silence.

The mind will always try to justify itself, to keep unhappiness and the self-image alive. Be the witness of all of this. Stop believing in whatever the mind does. It is all an illusion.

Just A Story

Part of not believing the mind is not believing in the story that it throws up around the emotions of depression. The reason for someone's depression is usually backed up with a story of what is currently happening in their lives. The story carries a negative energy, and is believed in, which gives it strength.

See that it is just a story! Just a collection of thoughts in the head – that is all. When you see that what seems to be causing you most harm is a story *created within your own mind* – you will not be so troubled by depression. Take a step back from the story-generator that is your mind – it is just forming a story that could be told many other ways.

If you drop all the mental commentary and story-telling, you will likely be left with a feeling of depression – perhaps a heaviness or a sadness. Feel these feelings fully without mentally labeling anything – just directly feel them. Then totally accept they are there as if you have chosen to feel them. See what happens.

Recognise The Futility

How has depression helped you? What useful purpose has it served? All depression does is maintain a false sense of self, tied to unhappiness, heaviness and suffering.

Can you see this clearly? Can you observe the depression within you and see that it is actually useless? That it only causes you to suffer? Can you be aware that something inside must *enjoy* feeling depressed? If you can, then remain observing in this way. As depression arises, do not take it seriously. You can even laugh at it, since you now realise how pointless it all is.

Something is producing depression inside you, somehow enjoying it, only serving to create suffering and to create a false self-image. Is this not strangely amusing? Do not get involved with the ridiculous emotions, just let them be and smile at their futility. They serve you no purpose, so give them no importance.

The observing consciousness that you are is already at peace, quiet and still. Infinite and indestructible, the silent awareness is your true nature and is the only constant thing in the universe – and it is who you are.

Thoughts, emotions, things, possessions, people, your body and personality all come and go, within your silent awareness. Remain only as this awareness, and let everything else come and go.

How To Deal With Depression Step-By-Step

1) Totally accept the feelings of depression as if you have chosen that they be there.

2) Do not run or hide from your feelings. Feel them fully from a place of unconditional acceptance.

3) Be the awareness of it, the space surrounding it that is untouched by depression.

4) Then you will not care if the depression is there or not, you are already surrendered and at peace. Gradually or suddenly, the depression will dissolve.

Much of this may seem totally counter-intuitive or even crazy, but that is why it is so effective, it makes no sense to the mind that creates suffering. Try the simple steps above as an experiment.

Ruthlessly accept your inner state *at this moment only.*

How To Transcend Suffering

"Most of our suffering comes when we want things to be different. If you are stressed, you suffer because you want the feeling to be different, if you feel sad, anxious, dark, lonely – all these things have power when you wish they were gone, or wish they were different.

Instead of fighting or objecting, just look at your feelings in the face, without trying to change them. Paradoxically, once you stop demanding they be different, their troublesome quality diminishes."

Suffering Is Not Who You Are

Suffering is not who you are. When any negative emotion, thought or suffering arises, know that it is nothing to do with you. Do not identify. Let it *be* completely. Be the space for it. Welcome it willingly, as if you have chosen the experience. From here you are automatically free through your acceptance, and as a result the suffering that is arising will diminish far quicker.

Do not be concerned about how long suffering will last or stay with you. If you want it to go, this is a form of resistance, which actually holds it in place. Paradoxically, suffering will last far less long if you practice total acceptance. It can be an enjoyable experiment – welcome your suffering as if it is pleasure.

This is a totally different way of treating suffering than we are used to – we are used to trying to resist or think our way out of negative emotional sates, or distracting ourselves with something else such as food, TV or other people.

Disrespect

We tend to have a great respect and give great importance to what makes us suffer, and we ignore our own freedom as a result. We give away so much of our power by blindly taking the mind to be true. If there is suffering inside, let it be there, but don't honour it, don't touch it, don't involve yourself. Be aware that without your existence, the suffering could not exist. It depends on you.

The Mind Is Your Teacher

We often hear spiritual phrases like "escape from your mind" or "break free from your mind". Often the thinking mind that causes us suffering is portrayed to be something bad or undesirable. While in a way this is true, never treat your mind to be something bad. It is a fantastic teacher, if you know how to understand its teaching.

The mind forces you out of identification with it by causing you distress. You are forced to simply remain as the awareness of it – since the suffering eventually becomes unbearable and any resistance makes it worse.

It is like the mind says: "If you identify with me, you will suffer. Your only way out of this suffering is to leave me be".

Realise The Truth

The suffering of the mind forces you to realise the truth – that you are the eternal, peaceful awareness silently observing thoughts, emotions and sense perceptions, not interfering with anything.

Leave The Mind Alone

Whenever the mind causes any pain or suffering within you, treat it as if it is saying to you: "leave me alone, I am just passing through, I am not real!" or "if you believe in 'me' you will get hurt, leave me be, leave me alone!".

When you go out and interact with the mind, hold its hand, get involved – it does not like it and it hits you in retaliation. This is your lesson – leave the mind alone, and it can do you no harm.

Who Is Suffering?

Locate the sufferer. Whoever it is that suffers physical or emotional pain – locate him or her. Can they be found? Are they a tangible entity? Keep looking and you will find no one. Suffering arises, but the sufferer of it is an illusion. It is the false self-image, the person in the body, the ego itself.

You Are Not The One Suffering, So Leave It Alone

Even the one that says "I am suffering" or "I hate this feeling" is the ego. The feeling of "I am suffering" is just another object in the space of your awareness. Leave it alone, let it be.

The one who *wants* or *tries* to transcend suffering is not the one who transcends it. You are already transcendent, as the effortless unmoved silence in which all of this appears.

Non Judgement = Freedom

To transcend suffering, do not judge your feelings or emotions, just be totally present with them and accept them. Your awareness and acceptance will disidentify you from the pain and will instantly end your suffering (as you are no longer resisting). From here you will not be concerned about how long uncomfortable feelings or emotions will stay with you – and as a result they will leave much quicker.

There is an unaffected space in which suffering is perceived. You are the space, not the suffering. Be the space.

Suffering Wakes You Up

Suffering forces you to go deeper into yourself and deeper into the present moment. It forces you out of identification with your mind and body. Either transcend suffering or remain identified with it.

Be grateful for your suffering. It is waking you up.

How To Forgive

"Forgiveness helps you more than anyone else. Through unforgiveness, you are the one who suffers most through holding on to resentment and hostility."

The mind often tells us that forgiveness is hard, forgiveness is difficult. What a lie this is. It is far more difficult to carry around the burden of hostility, regret or unforgiveness. To carry the weight of unforgiveness is a true difficulty, but it is a challenge that the mind is addicted to. So it says "it's hard to forgive or let go". This is a lie, a complete lie.

Once we recognise the addiction to unforgiveness, the strange enjoyment of burdens, we need not make an effort to "forgive" – we see that all of this drama is the creation of a dysfunctional mind.

Forgiving Others

If we speak about forgiving "other people" for what they have done, there are a few options. The first is to see that other people only exist in your imagination. The identity you form of another person only exists in your mind. It is the mind's fake representation of reality. In the same way that the mind creates an illusory identity of a person, of a "me" - it does this for every other body, it assigns each body a label and personality, feelings of like and dislike, stories of actions etc. If this is seen, then there is no one to forgive.

The other option is to fully be with all of your unforgiveness, hostility, regret, etc. and simply allow it to be there. Notice that it claims to be useful, but look to see how useful it actually is. Is it actually just a drain of energy and an upkeep of suffering? How does it serve you? It only keeps your false identity alive, it actually serves you in no way. Seeing the futility of holding on to unforgiveness means you need do nothing more. In this seeing, its power is weakened.

Don't force anything, if you can't forgive someone, accept it. Anything you allow and accept can not hold power over you. We often enter mental torture when we can not forgive but believe that we should. When you do not try to explain away the negative feelings, when you don't wish they be gone, you no longer feed them, they are exposed as pointless, just excess baggage.

The Madness Of Clinging To The Past

If there is an event that has passed, that is no longer present in your life, then why are you still even thinking about it? A better question would be: is it *you* who is still thinking about it? Find out for yourself – can you witness the thoughts of the past events arising? Can you witness the "me" that feels wronged, betrayed or hard-done by? Can you witness the emotions that come with the story and mind identity?

If you can witness these things, then are they really who you are? You are the pure silent witness, so remain as that for a moment. Let the feelings and thoughts of the past be there, but do not identify with these things, since they will come and go. Remain as the witness.

Be aware of the space that the story of the past arises within. Is the space affected? Is it moved or upset? Does it even care about the mental/emotional story? Be fully aware of this still, silent space that your internal dialogue arises within. Give your full attention to this space, since this space will not leave you or harm you.

If you fully believe in the story that your mind tells you about a past event, then forgiveness is very difficult. True forgiveness comes from beyond the mind, where the sense of separation and personal identity do not exist. The reason forgiveness seems so hard is because the mind has taken over.

Forgiveness will often not make sense to the mind. As long as the mind has a story of "me", "he", "she" or "they", then it has an identity, an occupation to keep it alive. The mind does not want to forgive, it does not want to let go, because this means its stories and identities will be brought to an end. Notice how the mind loves to hold on to pain and non-forgiveness. Do not be fooled by the mind! Go beyond it and dwell as the space in which it arises.

Then forgiveness is not even necessary, since the story is no longer given authority. Rather than a "me" having to forgive someone else, you realise that the past has no effect on you, no power over you, so there is nothing to forgive.

Forgiving Oneself

The true meaning for forgiving oneself is to no longer judge yourself. To simply allow yourself to be as you are. Allow your feelings and thoughts to be as they are, without believing they should be different. If you feel uncomfortable in any way, simply allow yourself to feel like this, allow the experience as it is. This is self-forgiveness, and paradoxically burns away or at least allows you to transcend the dysfunctions in the body and psyche. Once you are no longer feeding them through resistance or identification, they fall away.

Forgiving Your Past Actions

The phrase of "me forgiving myself" is a common one. Yet, it does not make sense. Who is the "me" forgiving, and who is the "myself" that is being forgiven?...

They are both concepts. Fictions of the mind. Both of these "selves" come from thoughts and imagination. You are the witness of both.

These self-concepts arise when we identify with the actions of our bodies and minds, and when we believe in the reality of the past. The past has passed, identifying with it is to create a false identity, or in other words – to hold on to the ego in you. Leave the past alone, it does not want to be touched.

You are here, witnessing all that arises. Realise this for yourself, and see that what you thought needed forgiveness is just a collection of thoughts that were previously given power through your own identification.

This is true forgiveness – seeing that what you thought needed forgiveness, is not real.

If you still feel you simply "can't forgive yourself", then fine – leave it at that. Don't feed it anymore or believe you should forgive yourself. Leave it alone. Let unforgiveness fend for itself. Notice how a part of the mind enjoys clinging to misery and painful stories. If the mind and emotions still wish to create suffering for themselves, this is no longer your problem. It cannot be controlled, so why be so interested in something that just creates pain? Realising the futility of the behaviours of the mind will lead to automatic transcendence.

How To Forgive The Present

How to forgive something or someone right now? Maybe someone is acting a certain way, doing a certain thing that seems harmful, manipulative, selfish etc. For any helpful change to occur, the best thing you can do is to instantly accept what is happening.

Acceptance puts you in a certain amount of inner freedom, inner peace and spaciousness. You are not carrying any drama or negativity. You instantly become aligned with Life.

Then, as if by magic, your body is moved to action if it is necessary. It may not be moved, and you may simply remain quiet.

Your reaction or words may surprise you from this place of inner acceptance. They become very effective, yet do not carry such a heavy sense of "I, the doer". It is just spontaneous action of the universe happening through you. It is not reactive. It is pro-active.

Seeing Sleepwalkers

Forgiving someone in the present moment is realising that their harmful behaviour is not who they are in truth. Their conditioning has completely taken over, and it is as if they are now sleepwalking.

If someone was sleepwalking and began to verbally abuse you, if you knew they were sleepwalking you may not even take it personally. You certainly would be able to forgive them quite easily, since you would see that they do not know what they are doing.

Being taken over by the ego is not much different. The only way you can see this, however, is to not be in the cage of your own mind, or personal self. Maintain a sense of inner spaciousness, emptiness. An awareness of silence or space even while your mind is thinking is very helpful. An awareness of the formlessness of your own Self will mean that you can recognise that in another. If you are totally inside "the person" in your mind, you will identify with your mind's reactions to the "other person".

From emptiness, anything you do carries a sense of forgiveness, of love. This does not mean that forceful action cannot be taken; it just means the vibration of the force is very high and pure, not messy and personal. It will happen naturally and carry no inner negativity or inner resistance.

The Storyless Space

Forgiveness is in leaving the mind behind. Don't trust the stories. Go into the space in which mind arises. In this storyless space – what is there to forgive? Get out of the imagination of past, future and even present, and realise that this timeless space is all there ever is.

Part 3

Discovering Freedom

As we continue to discard the futility of trying to feel different, see the uselessness of self-condemnation, we find ourselves no longer in conflict with ourselves or the world. The turbulent energies begin to dissolve, we become aware of a deeper stability, that which is unmoved by the thoughts and emotions that come and go...

The Futility Of Regret

"A ridiculous habit of ours, which will actually maintain the very energy that creates undesirable actions in the first place."

Regret is no doubt one of the most ridiculous of mankind's traits. He/she takes it on themselves to decide what was right and what was wrong, and then perpetuates the emotion of regret with its associated repetitive thoughts, with the unconscious belief that regret will resolve the matter.

In what way does regret serve a useful purpose? Learning from so-called "mistakes" is not the same as regret. If one wished, one could accept an apparent error, learn from it, and be done. Regret is different. Regret is a cheat, posing to be an honest friend.

All that is needed is to see the futility of regret. See how it only serves to create suffering, and to enhance a certain mental identity. It does not change the past, yet still claims to be of use and importance. Dare we not believe in regret when it arises? Can we realise its futility?

Accept the energetic presence of regret, but see its calls for belief and attention to be meaningless and laughable.

Notice that regret is strangely both hated and enjoyed at the same time. The Painmaker has emerged, reveling in the negativity and self-condemnation.

If there are uncomfortable feelings of "what I have done in the past", then simply be with them, let them be, do not resist. The mind will say that this allowance is not easy, but this is because the mind is addicted to negativity, it does not want the burden to be gone. It wants to eat away at the idea of the personal self. Allowance resolves this. It both heals the energy of regret, along with the behavioral tendency that may cause undesirable action to re-occur. This is not a "cop-out", it is not saying that "it doesn't matter what I do since I can just accept it" - no, it is deeper than that, it is energetic, it is healing the useless, it is dissolving what creates pain inwardly and outwardly. It takes you deeper into peace, into consciousness.

Our society (a product of the madness of the human mind) strongly believes in the effectiveness of punishment, rather than understanding and healing the root dysfunctions that lead to atrocities. Since we are trained to believe in punishment, we give great belief to the mind that creates the idea of "me and what I have done" and then punishes it through harmful thinking. It can even take this punishment stance if there is nothing to regret - for example if there is a trait in the personality that the mind labels as "bad". Set aside the self-punishment mentality. Re-habilitate through surrender, non-avoidance of inner pain, and allowance.

Eradicating Guilt

"Guilt wants to keep you down, keep you trapped, keep you dwelling in painful stories. Does guilt actually serve any useful purpose?"

Guilt can be one of the mind's favourite tricks to keep you stuck in identity and in time. It is also one of the most seductive and addictive tendencies that humans tend to have.

Guilt can claim to come for many reasons. This chapter will mostly deal with guilt of hurting others, intentionally or unintentionally.

We are brought up being told that guilt is justified. To not feel guilty about something "done wrong" is often seen as inhuman, irresponsible or selfish. We are also engrained with the sense of doership – that whatever the body says or does, "I" am the doer.

Yet does guilt help? Or does it just create further suffering? Does long-term guilt actually teach us anything useful, or just keep us trapped in a negative state that actually contributes to negative actions? Noticing the futility of guilt, that it actually serves no useful purpose, can be very helpful for freedom from it.

Expressing Guilt

If you suffer from guilt, you have two options. The first is to talk with whoever is involved. Explanation, apology, expression of feelings – all these things help to release the inner turmoil of guilt. You may notice that whenever you apologise or express your feelings of guilt, you afterwards feel lighter, resolved, more balanced. Your natural state returns to the surface.

If, for whatever reason, you can not speak with the other

person, or if the guilt still lives on, then guilt can be transcended internally....

Transcending Guilt Internally

If you suffer from guilt, know that something inside loves to produce feelings of guilt. It loves the feeling, the story, the identity, the sense of separateness and self-condemnation. If you can be aware of this, you are removing your identity from the emotion of guilt.

Guilt will justify itself. It may even claim that the guilt is so strong because your love for another person is so strong. Almost as if your guilt is proof of your love for another. Do not give your belief to this.

All hindsight is futile, since you look to the past with different knowledge than you had at the moment of action. You then expect your past action to have been illuminated with the knowledge that you now have of events that came later. This is part of human madness.

How do you know what was really right or wrong? Put simply – you don't know. No one does. No one knows for sure what should or should not have happened. Each event you perceive is just a tiny yet intrinsic fragment of the whole. Human judgement is massively flawed, since it comes from a tiny, limited and often deluded perspective.

Intention?

If actions happened where you had the intentions to hurt another being, and later feel guilty about it – you can safely say that the entity acting was not your pure Self. It was the ego and its related tendencies. This is not a "cheat" way to absolve yourself of responsibility, but a truth.

The ego is blind. The pain it carries, it often seeks to place onto another. If it consumes you and you become identified with it, then it may use your body or mind to hurt another being. After this is done and the egoic energy is expressed and acted out, you no longer look through its eyes, and you realise what has happened. Your view is no longer infected by the "pain is good" assumption of the ego, and you realise the suffering that has been inflicted.

The extra pain for you then comes with the belief that *"the egoic energy that just acted through this body, was me. I had a choice. I had control over my actions, and I chose wrongly. I should have known better."* Is this true? Did you have control? Were you in a position to consciously choose how to act? Or did something else consume you and your thinking? Did some pain rise up that sought to create more pain?

The way to prevent harming others or carrying out actions that may lead to guilt, is to recognise the pain within you that seeks to harm yourself and others. Recognise its ignorance, its force, the way it tries to consume your body and mind. Be alert. Then allow its existence, but you need not contribute. Be the awareness of it, be the neutral empty space for it. Do not fight it or interpret it mentally with thoughts of "me" or "mine". This removes your identity and removes fuel from the painful energies. Feeling guilty will not prevent recurrence of a behaviour. Guilt will only make things worse.

If you harmed another unintentionally, but feel guilty about it, what is the point in that? You did not even have an intention to hurt another, so how can you be blamed?

Other Forms Of Guilt

Of course guilt can arise in other forms, such as guilt of non-action, or guilt of harbouring certain feelings. As a general guide I would say that much of our guilt comes from learning and conditioning, that it is a false emotion, not to be believed in. It does not help. Even if we think guilt will help us to take useful action or achieve things, the foundation of these actions will always be guilt instead of inspiration, enjoyment or intuition. As a foundation for action, guilt is a shoddy one, which is unlikely to hold up or actually sustain useful action.

The world will often try to make you feel guilty, since so may humans carry it around and want to dump it on others. We can even carry so much guilt that we believe we have to work to survive, to earn our place in the universe. Is there any other animal that believes this? Since we have isolated our sense of self from nature, we feel inherently guilty. Don't buy the guilt stories anymore. Offer no fight to guilt, go beyond, be the natural intelligence that is the source of all thoughts and sensations.

Healing Anger

"Anger in itself is fine. Let it come and go without involving yourself. When you identify with it, when you believe you are it, it becomes fuelled, perpetuates and pollutes the psyche and body."

There is nothing wrong with anger in itself. Again, like all emotions, it is energy. It causes suffering for us however, when it becomes personal, when it becomes attached to a story in the head of what is happening and what should be happening instead.

Usually we feel anger when outer events don't conform to the wishes of the personal mind. It believes that anger and resistance will help it get things the way it wants, and then it can be happy again. Notice that most of the time, our anger has this logic:

"I was feeling ok, but now 'this' is happening, which is not how it should be. Now I do not feel ok, I feel angry about it. My anger is because of this external event. For me to be at peace again, I must be free from this anger, and the only way to be free from this anger is for the external situation to be different..."

So we always tend to look to the external event to change before we can be at peace again. This is a kind of psychological enslavement, an addiction to and dependence on externals. Often this way of looking at things is seen as quite normal.

Rarely are we told that most of our anger comes from what the mind tells us *about* what is happening, rather than what is actually happening. Often it is based on concepts, conditioning and imaginary interpretations. In this way anger is no longer felt as an energy in the body that comes and goes, but becomes "my anger", it becomes "me" and consumes "me", and holds "me" hostage until things change externally.

Anger is fine, but when it consumes someone, they usually end up regretting their actions. The anger completely takes over, and often seeks to create more suffering rather than merely resolve a situation. Once the anger (or anything else negative) has acted out through someone and has somehow "got its fix" of suffering, then sanity arises again, and the person realises the senseless actions that have taken place.

How To Deal With Anger In Yourself

If you find yourself often getting angry about things, or with people, the first thing to notice is that something inside loves to get angry. It loves the drama, the inflated sense of self and separateness from the rest of the world, it even loves the suffering that ensues. It is an energy field that seeks to create more suffering, it is not who you are. Notice the addiction to suffering that it carries, and you will be able to naturally see that you are not the anger. Simply watch it. Notice how it also loves to take over thoughts, consuming the identity of "me" and creating many outraged stories about what is happening, what other people did or what others are doing. As an experiment, drop your belief in the thoughts that come. They are only thoughts. All is the energy of the Painmaker. It loves to feel disturbed.

Although on one level anger is enjoyed by the human dysfunction, it is also hated. We feel disturbed, and therefore want the anger to be gone. This makes things far worse. We feel internally molested, and the mind says that the reason for this inner trouble is other people or other things, that even though it tries to control, knows that it actually can't. What a tremendous burden of suffering, to believe your emotions are completely at the mercy of objects apparently alien to yourself.

Try not wanting the anger to be gone. Don't act as if it should not be there. Let it be there. Be with it. Feel it, but don't give your belief to it. Allow it. Instantly this removes a great deal of suffering. We get far more upset when we believe that any inner disturbance is some kind of offence that we don't deserve. Let it be there without trying to change it.

This allows you to go to the root cause of the anger, which is within you, not in some external circumstance. The source of anger is inside, and it claims that external events are the cause of it, in order to distract the attention from discovering the truth. The seed is always within. The seed is burnt once it is seen, identified as not who you are (since you can see it), and then not fought or argued with. Anger is an argument with Life, it is a resistance, a fight. To not fight anger means it cannot stay alive.

Anger may still come, flashes of it, perhaps it will still operate in mental stories for a while. This is fine. Don't call it "wrong" or "unspiritual". Gradually it is not even seen as anger anymore, the thoughts are not given automatic belief, and it is seen as nothing. It is not personal, so whether it is expressed outwardly or not is not up to "you" anymore, it is spontaneous.

How To Deal With Anger In Others

First notice how the individual has been consumed by this emotional energy. The Painmaker has taken them over, and they do not even realise. They are basically sleep walking, with something else possessing their mind. It is not who they are. Compassion arises more easily when you view anger in others in this way.

Let them be. They have a right to be angry if that is what they choose (everyone ultimately has a choice). If the moment requires speech or action on your part, you will find these things being done without any inner resistance or negativity from you. You do or don't do whatever the moment requires. It is as if the moment uses you for the benefit of itself, rather than you trying to change the moment into what you want it to be. This is conscious action, and comes from an inner nonresistance to what *is*. Life lives through you in this way, and you are the awareness behind all of it.

If you become identified with the anger arising in you, this feeds the anger. Anger will likely react through you and look to strengthen itself in another person as well.

Angry people may try to provoke you to react negatively to give their emotional state and sense of self a reality. Do no such thing. Why even entertain their madness? Just remain present, and their anger will sort itself out. Let the moment *be*, in whatever disguise it is in. Remember that right action emerges from this place of peace, not from personal resistance on your part.

All you can do is observe the other's Painmaker playing out, and observe your own inner state. You may still find reactions taking place inside you. So use this as a spiritual practice. Dissolve your ego through awareness and acceptance. You may be surprised at what effect this has on the situation when you are in this state. Things seem to resolve themselves quicker through nonresistance than when you get sucked into the drama and negativity.

Many people do not realise they have a choice not to be angry. Not many people are aware of how to deal with anger. When people are identified with their own anger, they tend to believe it is completely necessary and natural. They can not see the insanity of it. It makes perfect sense to the ego, so they also believe it makes perfect sense.

If you resist anger, you feed it. If you do not react, you give it no reality.

Anger usually stems from fear of the ego. It constantly fears loss or destruction. If it feels threatened (which it often does), anger is a common defense mechanism. Notice it in yourself and others. A simple noticing is enough to no longer feel as if you are trapped in it.

Anger Often *Creates* The Triggers

Separate the situation from your thoughts about it. Your thoughts are the main sources of pain. These thoughts are troublesome and deceptive, they create suffering, so why give them so much belief and importance?

Anger comes from inside you, not from outside you. The world merely shows you the anger that is already there. You may believe a situation makes you angry, but it is your reaction that makes you angry. The external situation just acts as a trigger for what is already in you. The external situation is just a reflection of your inner state.

We usually believe our anger and our resistance towards certain situations helps to resolve them, or that our potential for anger will somehow stop certain things happening. It seems that on a deeper level, this is a trick. The stored tendency for anger actually tends to create corresponding external events in the first place, so that the anger tendency can be triggered and maintained.

To go within, to realise the source of anger, to be aware of the emptiness from which it emerges, is to weaken the tendency and therefore weaken the outwards reflections in one's Life.

Treat this life as a cleansing process. Each moment shows you the illusions that still dwell inside you, so you can be freed from them.

Dissolving Fear

"Fear need not be feared. Stop pushing it away, denying it or fighting it. Fear is full of energy waiting to be allowed and accepted. Forget what you think you know about fear, and feel it for what it is."

We often hear, particularly within self-help or spiritual groups, that fear is not good. We often hear a lot about how fear is a limitation, something we should not be experiencing, something that we should be free of. Rather than debating all of this, let's just drop it for a moment. Forget the idea that you should be free from fear, or that fear should not arise in your experience. Don't push fear away or try to deny it.

Fear is powerful energy. Whenever we label it as wrong or bad, the energy becomes suppressed, congested, less useful. If we change our attitude to fear, and instead fully welcome it without having any opinions about it, it becomes extremely helpful. It gives us great energy. If the fear is due to a physical threat or a confrontation, fully allowing fear means we are not inhibited in our actions. The fear becomes an energy source rather than something that consumes us.

If the fear is useless, this doesn't matter. If we treat it the same way, by letting it be there, not running away from it, then the useless stuff loses its commanding power. Naturally it is seen as less serious, it is given less respect.

Naturally we seem to respect fear. Often we believe in all the thoughts tied to it, or tied to any other emotion, for that matter. To fully allow it to be there removes the resistive entity of an inner person, the one "trying to figure out" or "transcend" the emotions, and so the thoughts and energies in motion (e-motion) can not stick to anything inside. They pass through. They can stay for however long they want, there is no longer a "me" that is affected or dominated by them, no longer a person at the root that feels they are responsible for these feelings. Let these emotions fend for themselves, they do not require your maintenance.

<u>Undisturbed Being</u>

"You are the impersonal being, beyond description, untouched, out of which the feeling of being a man or a woman arises."

When everything is allowed, when you no longer believe you are the one responsible for the energies in the body, there is a relaxation, there is a surrender. Even the person inside that resists or argues with thoughts or emotions is allowed. In this allowance, we find that all of these feelings are arising in an untouched, impersonal space, an emptiness, without which nothing, including the thought of "I" could exist. In the same way that the space in a room is unaffected by the objects within it, the space of being is undisturbed by the energies arising in it. Everything that is arising in this space is not who you are, this is clear – so why give such importance or tie your sense of self to any of this content?

Discomfort may be there, for a while there may be feelings of heaviness or sadness, things not associated with ideas of inner peace or introspection. When we approach our inner state in an allowing, fearless way, what we are often not told is that all of the stale energies in the body that have been suppressed, are then released, so initially the feelings feel even stronger than when we were avoiding them! Thoughts and emotions seem to rebel at first, demanding respect and disturbance. Let them rebel, they are only as serious as you believe them to be.

We are so trained in avoidance. If we feel bored, we switch on the TV, if we feel dissatisfied, we eat something, if we feel lonely, we seek company. As much as possible, don't avoid any longer. Simply allow yourself to feel however you feel, there is nothing wrong. This theme of allowing yourself to feel however you feel has obviously been constant throughout the book, but I feel it has to be emphasised since it is the complete opposite to our conditioned response. Even though it may not seem the easy choice, it dissolves our inner disturbances at their root, freeing you from them, rather than making you dependent on some external to temporarily keep trouble at bay. Let inner trouble come!

As you become aware, through surrender, that there is an inner, untouched space of being, simply feel it. Feel how it feels, this emptiness or stillness, this sense of aliveness or being. It is not a dead "thing", it is Life itself. The only reason you do not experience this as yourself, is because the personal self of the mind consumes so much respect and attention. Yet, notice that this undisturbed space of being is not affected by the personal self. The true being is not a person or a personality, it is just pure being. Surrender to it, let it emerge fully, without making any demands.

We are also so trained in effort, in "making things happen" - you need not have this approach. Pure being can emerge more fully when the one "trying" to do everything is seen as just another thought or energy form, that has no real truth to it. From here a greater power can move into your Life, influencing action for the better.

Embracing Life Energy

*"Emotions are all the energy of Life. Resisting them keeps them dense
and strong. To heal them, we embrace them."*

Emotions carry the energy of life. They are all from the source
of consciousness. They play roles of good and bad, dense and
light, pleasant and unpleasant, but really they are all the same.
Be in equanimity, this is the secret. Treat good and bad alike.
Let them be, let them surge in the body. Without resisting
them, and without identifying with them (without taking
them to be who you are), they can cause no real disturbance.
They may create feelings – yes, but it is possible to be
undisturbed by them by no longer giving them value, by no
longer needing to fight or argue with them, and no longer
blaming yourself for the emotions that arise. Often they can
be collective, inherited or conditioned, which supports the
fact that they are not who you are.

If you feel heavily burdened with emotion or resistance,
hopefully this book, the basic "methods" of surrender, inner
yielding, nonjudgement and awareness, will help heal the
emotional pain. Do not be fooled when emotions seem to get
worse – they are just being released, coming up and therefore
being felt more intensely. Let them come, take no
responsibility. Gradually they become released, there is more
lightness, and the tendency for reactivity is dissolved. Using
this same approach will also prevent burial or suppression of
any new emotions that arise. No longer fight them. Let these
energies *be*.

However troublesome the mind or emotions may be, they
think they are doing what's best. On some level these energies
believe they are helpful, of benefit. Therefore you need never
fight your emotions, or try to wrestle or out-think the mind. If
anything, treat these energies with compassion – they know
no better.

Be aware of yourself as that in which emotion moves, that awareness which is always present, whether emotion is there or not. Be yourself in this way.

No longer treat emotions personally, whether from yourself or another. Witness them instead. Act like you don't know what they are for, as if you do not know their reason for being. Then whatever is in service to the moment will shine forth as truth, as knowing, and the rest will naturally be discarded. Live in peace, as peace itself.

The Stages And Process Of Emotional Healing

At the time of writing this, it has been a number of years since the book has been released. I thought I would add an extra chapter to answer any questions or address any issues that arise when I speak with people during one-to-one sessions about this topic. We will start with the basic stages of emotional healing that people often go through during the emotional healing process, and then we will address some "troubleshooting issues"...

This chapter will act as a summary of the entire book.

Stage 1 - Awareness, Noticing The Emotion Is Not Who You Are

The first stage of emotional healing is always to see that in fact, whatever you experience, whatever comes and goes, is not really who you are. Our habit is to assume that every time I feel angry, hateful, resentful, anxious, afraid, jealous good or bad or anything else, then it is *me* and it is *my fault*. Not only do we often take our thoughts and feelings to be who we are, but we also believe that we are the ones generating these things on purpose.

It is a very significant thing to *notice* emotions and thoughts, rather than thinking you *are* them or thinking you are trapped *inside* of them.

With this said, people can often fall into a trap of forming a sense of self that feels as if it is an object that is watching other objects - a little ball of "me" which desperately tries to watch and stay vigilant and distance itself from any unwanted thoughts and emotions.

We are often trained to view life through a dense ball of resistance called "me". When we notice that emotions aren't who we are, because they come and go, rise and fall while we remain here, sometimes people can then "look" at emotions from this same dense ball of resistance inside, perhaps somewhere in the head or behind the eyes.

Luckily, this dense ball is also another feeling, another sensation, that is in fact *effortlessly* noticed.

Our thinking minds can not understand that something can be observed by nothing. We assume that if we are aware of something, then the awareness must be a *thing* as well. It must be a person. It must have a shape and a feeling and a denseness. In truth, this isn't true. Have no assumptions about what awareness really is. Notice that anything that feels as if it is you, is *arising in you*. If this starts to feel confusing, it just shows that our minds are not capable of grasping this through thinking. Don't worry about understanding any of this at all.

With all of that said, the first stage in the emotional healing process is no longer assuming that emotions are who you are in essence.

Stage 2 - Yielding, or Acceptance

It is certainly possible to feel aware of a painful emotion, and yet still have a strong resistance to it. It is only normal. We are always trained to fight and resist what is not desirable, in the hope that the resistance will fix things. Certainly on an inner level, the resistance creates a tension that seems to hold what we do not want in place.

Then, someone can hear about the benefits of yielding or not resisting or accepting the emotion, letting it be exactly as it is. If this is done so that eventually they can get rid of this annoying emotion that they are *secretly resisting*, then they may end up frustrated because it isn't working how they want it to.

It often helps to be very experimental, or playful. What would happen if I let this feeling be whatever the hell it wants to be, so that it isn't my responsibility to manage it anymore? How would it feel to yield to this resistance inside of me? How would it feel to be without this resistance to myself, just for a moment?

If you approach things like this hypothetically, you can let yourself off the hook. Things aren't so heavy. You can even try the hypothetical approach with repetitive negative thought patterns or emotions. For example - how would it feel to not need to be angry at this? You then leave a space. You feel it out. Then you can notice not only how you feel, but what you gain or lose by being without a certain draining emotion. How do I benefit, or how am I losing out on something? Often you might find you are not hindered by letting something go, and that in fact through treating it hypothetically ("What if?"), you show to yourself that when you treat yourself and your feelings lightly, things can be released far more easily than when you were fighting against what you didn't like within your mind and body. This leads us to the final stages of the emotional healing process...

Stage 3 - Does the Emotion or Thought Pattern Serve You?

Once something has been given space, once it is allowed to be exactly as it is, we can look at it more fairly, and see what it is doing for us. Often things feel as if they have a hold over us internally, because we feel that on some level they are helping us. Perhaps they are, perhaps they have, but perhaps now they are no longer needed.

If we identify what a thought or emotion is trying to do for us, then often that leads to a greater sense of lightness, love and compassion for it. It is doing its best, as best it knows how. Lets give an example:

A man has an argument with his boss at work. He comes home, angry and dull, and he can't seem to stop thinking about what was said, how outrageous and unfair his boss was, what he should have said to his boss, what he wanted to say but didn't, what he thinks would be good to say now but can't. He comes home, sits, down, and drives himself mad.

Often anything like this, any repetitive emotional loop that harms us, often feels as if it is leading us away from itself, as if to offer a way out of the thinking through more thinking. We seek a way out, an end to the cycle, but we make the cycle stronger.

When the man has had enough, and realises he simply can't stop thinking about all of this, feeling so angry, he can start by just noticing the force of it, the surge of energy and power that is inside his head, his body, everywhere. He just notices.

Through just noticing, he is already accepting, he does not have to try to accept. He just notices, emptily, without ideas or opinions.

Then ideas and opinions rise up, ideas about how he is feeling vs how he should be feeling, ideas of how he doesn't want to feel this way at all.

Again, he just notices it all. He notices resistance, the shouts of the mind, without adding any more resistance to it.

Then, he notices the purpose of all of it. He realises that he is sat alone in a room, and that his boss is nowhere to be seen. He realises that all these feelings are doing is sucking his attention into a bad dream, and that they are not reaching out into his life and creating any better situation for him.

And then perhaps the emotions and thoughts flare up in response to this.

"If you don't think about this you won't be able to stand up for yourself."

"If you don't think about this then it will just happen again."

"If you don't think about this then you won't be prepared next time."

All kinds of justifications for negativity will arise, and again, he notices them. He notices that whether these reasons are true or not, that the intentions, even if fictional, are trying to protect him. They are all based around him being safer in the future, avoiding some kind of pain. Often all of our negative feelings are based around this - they are unconscious attempts to help us avoid pain, death, or something going wrong in the future.

The man breathes a sigh of relief. These energies have the intention of helping him. Whether they are really helping or not is a different matter, but at least they have the intentions of helping.

Things soften a little. There is some space. He continues to notice that despite their justifications and intentions, these negative, painful feelings are not improving his work situation, his boss or his abilities to speak freely. They are just consuming his attention, making himself feel even more stuck in something he doesn't want to be in.

And then, he realises that he is giving all of his power away to a boss he doesn't like, to a situation he isn't fond of. He is inflating it without knowing it, making it stronger in his life. He notices that he is not helping himself though creating pain for himself. He does not *tell himself* this, he *notices it* there in the moment.

Then he relaxes a little further, and he has far more space to focus on the kind of boss he would like, or the kind of career that would be ideal for him. And this is the most effective agent for change. Your focus shifts away from what you hate, and into what feels good. Attention is energy. Whatever you feed with attention, grows, and the other things whither away.

With that said, later when he cooks himself a meal, his boss pops back in his head again. The argument comes back. Instead of saying "Oh no! There's that feeling again! It shouldn't be there! I thought I let it go!" he has less expectations of himself and his feelings, and instead the voices and thoughts sound like petulant children, dying energies that are screaming for food. He smiles, and makes his own meal.

This brings up another point about the stages of emotional healing...

Expectations Will Bring You Down

At any stage, if a feeling arises and you have expected yourself to never experience it again, then suddenly this emotion is huge in your life, in your world, in your mind. It seems like a big deal, when really it is nothing.

If we lessened our expectations about what thoughts we should and should not experience, then we wouldn't even have the time to pay attention to the ones that bring us down or make us uncomfortable. We would naturally be suited towards peace, and less interested in fighting with old disturbances.

Emotions Are Not Bad

This is a common theme in the book. We can have a glorified idea that we should be emotionless, no longer human if we are evolved spiritually. Again, the truth of this doesn't really matter, but the *idea of it* can destroy your peace of mind. A sage would not care what kinds of emotions arise. They are not personal. They are not measures of who you are. Emotions can have a purpose - even anger has a purpose at times. As long as we are not in conflict with ourselves, then we can remain conscious, and emotions are naturally used for our benefit and the benefit of the situation.

Resistance Is Not To Be Resisted

Resistance is not bad either. If you find there is great resistance to your own feelings, simply notice the resistance, and offer no resistance to it.

"It's Getting Worse. Am I Doing It Wrong?"

During the emotional healing process, it is likely that things will return. I myself suffered a while with intense anger and frustration, massive heat in the body in certain social or isolated situations. There was a great deal of pent up energy and frustration from people or the world not meeting my expectations, but suppression of certain emotions because I didn't want to hurt people or make situations worse. This Painmaker energy, even after made conscious, survived for a long while after, and at first, got even more intense.

"Why is this getting worse now if I'm aware of it?"

"It feels even more painful. Am I doing it wrong? I must be!"

"Am I not accepting this enough? Why is it getting worse?"

This happens with a lot of people. They manage to notice emotions, rather than being fully dragged in, but then experience emotional pain worse than ever. There are a few reasons, perhaps, why this is:

Since you are more conscious, you are more sensitive. You can feel something more acutely, rather than just being taken over and blinded by it.

The Painmaker energy or thought energy is used to your belief, interest, identification and attention. If this starts to be removed, it can flare up to be more easily fed. It can try to create confusion to pull your attention back into chaos, and into resisting it. It is like someone who is desperate for a fight, so much so that they start to beat you. On an internal level, with your own emotions, turn the other cheek. "Resist not evil" when it comes to your own thoughts and feelings. Let your mind hit you, so to speak. Be a punch bag for thoughts, and you will notice that you lose your solidity.

As something is released, it is felt more intensely. Something has been below the surface for a while, coming up to feed every now and again. As it comes up to feed, it is not met with the food of your interest and resistance, and it comes up further to look for food. It looks and looks and comes up more and more, and as it is released out of you, it is felt in its fullness, in its purity, and so it feels more intense. Take it as part of the release process. As something is felt more strongly, it is being released.

Do You Deserve It? Do They Deserve It? Does The Situation Deserve It?

A final tip to help with the emotional healing process, is to question whether the object of your pain deserves it.

Does the person really deserve your anger or your thoughts? Does the situation deserve your anxiety? Do you deserve to suffer?

The last one might bring up some surprising answers. On some level, we can be conditioned to believe that we DO deserve to suffer, or that suffering is valid in certain situations. Uncovering these beliefs in oneself is the first stage. Then it is up to you to see if it is really true - are you sure you deserve it? How can you be sure?

With all of this, it is very helpful to not be too sure of things - not sure about how you should feel, not sure what your painful thoughts mean, not sure if they should be there or not, not sure if your thoughts are to be trusted. The uncertainness creates space. When we are certain of how we should feel, who we are, what our thoughts mean - then when we are experiencing negativity we can begin to feel stuck. All of the mental certainty creates a rigidness or a hardness. There is tremendous value in realising you don't actually know for sure how you should be feeling. It creates space for self-forgiveness, or self allowance.

Be aware that all of your emotions consist of your own energy. If you are focused on something or someone negatively in your life - do they deserve your precious energy?

The Universal Intelligence.

A final final tip. Sometimes you might feel that despite this book, despite the videos or meditations or advice on the same topic - it all still feels useless. You still feel as if you are suffering. There is one more thing you can try, if it resonates with you.

Open up to the universe for help. You might have a different word for it - God, Nature, The Whole, Infinite Intelligence. If it is anything for you, simply open up and ask for help. Hand some responsibility over as to how you feel and how you should be feeling. Let God take the burden and the care and the responsibility. Treat all experience as if it is the will of the universe at that moment, and see what happens.

If there are ever any more bonus chapters that are added to this book, I would like to let you know so that you can read them free of charge. An easy way to be notified of any additions is to **sign up to my free Sunday Wisdom newsletter** below. There is no spam, just some valuable weekly wisdom with a similar feel to this book, along with any updates and news of extra things you can get. **You also get a free eBook of** my conversations with people on this topic, perhaps answering any questions you might have.

Sign up and get the free eBook using the link below:

www.innerpeacenow.com/sunday-wisdom-inner-peace-ebook

I hope this has been valuable for you in shedding some light on the stages of emotional healing and can help you in the emotional healing process. If you can be so aligned with yourself that you aren't even wishing anything away - this is the greatest atmosphere for healing. I'd love to hear your feedback.

All the best to you,

Adam

About The Author

Thank You For Reading.

Did you find this book useful? If you did, **I would hugely appreciate it if you could leave a quick review** to **help the book** reach more people. It signals to others that the book is a trustworthy source of knowledge, and it also acts as a **great feedback** for me and my work.

If you can **spare a few seconds, please leave a quick review** on the book's Amazon page.

Just type in "Adam Oakley Undisturbed" in Amazon, and it should come up for you.

Thank you for doing this!

More About Me

If you enjoyed this book, I have a few websites and more books you can check out...

I am the author of the website **www.InnerPeaceNow.com**, which is a free resource for uncovering the peace within. It contains articles, meditations and some videos to help you on your journey.

I also carry out **one-to-one sessions** with people online who would like help working through issues, releasing painful patterns and experiencing more inner peace. Feel free to book a session with me using the website above if you are interested.

Books

Here are some more books by me that you might find useful on your journey. All are available on Amazon and also through my website www.InnerPeaceNow.com in other eBook formats...

"Get Out Of The Cage: A Guide To Inner Freedom"

"Inner Peace Sessions: Responses To Questions From Readers and Callers on InnerPeaceNow.com"

Fiction

Mythical Creatures Of The Forest

The Work Of Ronald Berkley: A Novella To Realise Your Power

Happiness Is Inside: 25 Inspirational Stories For Greater Peace Of Mind

Fighting For Freedom: A Slavery Story

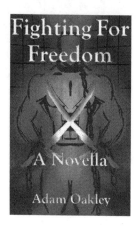

Poetry

Inner Peace Poetry

- - - - -

Thank you for purchasing this book, I hope it has been of use to you, and has shown you the power of simply facing all feelings, without wishing they be gone. No longer fear any sensation, you are far greater than anything that arises in you. Pay attention to yourself, that space in which all thoughts, emotions and sensations can come and go.

64204574R00062

Made in the USA
Middletown, DE
28 August 2019